Cowboys of the High Sierra

Cowboys
of the High Sierra

by Peter Perkins

Introduction by Dee Brown

NORTHLAND PRESS / FLAGSTAFF, ARIZONA

Frontispiece: Many cowboys will say that horses are working tools of the trade, and that you can't make pets out of them. But in 1840, a Texan described his feelings in another way: "When mounted on a noble animal, our concepts are bold, and we feel nerved for feats of high daring; but astride a scrub, our mental operations are spiritless and creep as sluggishly as the dull animal we are riding."

Right: On the Onyx Ranch in Kern County, the southernmost part of the Sierra, a "Nighthawker" trots across the moon-punctuated sky below Butterbread Peak. Mark Dalton told of nighthawking: of dozing in the saddle on night guard while listening to the lead cowbell. When the sound became too far away, he'd wake up and round 'em up. The image has long been romanticized. Cowboy artist Charlie Russell painted himself as young Nighthawker in his Laugh Kills Lonesome; *Frederic Remington painted an equally famous Nighthawker in his* Stampeded by Lightning.

Overleaf: Duane Anderson cowboyed in Wyoming for a number of years before coming to Likely, California, the birthplace of his wife and their family. "I thought we might be able to start a ranch out here," says Duane, "but land costs even more here, so it doesn't look too likely for us in Likely. I guess we'll be movin' on."

To the memory of

Frederic Remington
Hubert H. Bancroft
Edward S Curtis

Contents

Preface

THIS BOOK IS ABOUT COWBOYS who are raising cattle in the Sierra Nevada Mountains. It is not a story about the past but about the ongoing life story of working cowboys today. I sought them out because I was interested in their lifestyle. My ancestors were pioneer people who came to California across the plains in covered wagons four generations ago. Some of them were cowboys. I went to the Monache Rodeo to photograph a story for *Outside Magazine* and became so impressed

Left: Shoshone, Paiute, and Mono Indians hunted the Sierra hills, home of deer, rabbit, and bird. The Indians washed their acorns in this very river, the South Fork of the Kern. Indian cowboy Tommy Jefferson tells of the Depression years of the thirties: "My father, a Mono Indian, with a small hunting party would hunt all summer in the High Sierra for deer that the women would make into jerky for the tribe to eat in the winter. I've heard people say that if it weren't for my father, the tribe would have starved. My mother tells me that those days were the happiest ones, that the tribe was a unit then, working together. She was a very resourceful woman, enduring many hardships in silence."

with the wisdom of the cowboys and their strength as individuals that I wanted to create a book about their lives. Through them I came to know more about my grandfathers and great-grandfathers and more of myself.

My aim in this book is to portray the cowboy as he really exists, both in photographs and by recording conversations I had with each of them. The stories in this book are in the cowboys' own words; the combination of photographs and oral histories offers a depth that neither words nor photos have separately. I want to demonstrate how the cowboy works and lives and thinks about himself as a part of nature. He is a rugged, dynamic individualist whose artistic and philosophic expression is demonstrated in his very lifestyle. His fierce determination to hold on through tough years of drought, disease, and depressed cattle markets only exemplifies his love for his cowboy culture. The cowboy is something of a "John Henry" with a horse instead of a hammer. He whistles "A man ain't nothin' but a man"

[ix]

while doin' it the old way on horseback. As Sandy Kemp states, "I'm not very fancy.... You don't need a lot of fancy stuff." But unlike John Henry, Sandy Kemp is a millionaire and he has a choice. And as Fletcher Christensen tells it in Likely, California, "We have a close little community here. We respect each other. If a neighbor needs any help he usually can get it. The guy with fifty cents in his pocket or the guy with one hundred thousand all look alike and dress alike and think alike and talk alike and all do the same kind of work. It's just a lifestyle...." Of the hundreds of cowboys I met, not one said, "I'd rather be doing something else but this is all I know how to do." They all have other trades: carpentry, masonry, truck driving, and mechanics; and a good many also have a college education. John Lacey is a few credits short of a Master's degree. Scott Kemp has a degree from UCLA. Fletcher Christensen and Pearce Flournoy have had several years of college, and Doug Mullen spent two years at Cal Poly before his riding horses indoors and shooting out lightbulbs convinced the college faculty that perhaps Doug had best start ranch life without benefit of a degree. As cowboy Buck Bills, who has been forced into other trades as butchering and road-grading because of drought and depression, says, "I'll tell you, there ain't no bigger excitement in this life than runnin' full-tilt alongside of a wild horse and droppin' a loop around his neck. That's it for me! There ain't nothin' more excitin' to me."

The characters in this book are not a bunch of country bumpkins who are unaware of the twentieth century. They are a viable economic work force of aware people who have made a choice to remain with the old ways simply because they find that this affords a better quality of life. The cowboy following the axiom "Fix it yourself or go broke" makes his ranch a challenging place for inventive design under the pressures of necessity and scarce materials. He's a conservationist through heritage. He makes do. The grandfathers of these Sierra cowboys came west in the middle to late 1800s from the South and the Midwest and the post-Civil War depression. Most had very little. They all had agrarian backgrounds. After an attempt at the mines, most went to raising cattle in the High Sierra just as their grandsons do today. Not much has changed. Modern times have brought the pickup and cattle trucks, but fancy air conditioning units and electric blankets still have not replaced a good warm quilt or a favorite shade tree.

The Sierra Nevada range is five million years old and is California's largest natural resource. It offers a vast recreation area for hikers, campers, hunters, and fishers as well as hosting such businesses as forestry, mining, farming, and sheep and cattle ranching. A great

Right: With the cows headed for home and the marketplace, the critical moment of realizing the profits from the year's work will soon arrive. Profit is calculated on the weight of the animal; with good water and feed, good profits are the general rule. But when the Sierra snowpack is light, the spring runoff does not nourish the meadows; much in the life of the cowboy is in the hands of nature. Notice the ears on that horse — that horse is a mule. Her name is Dolly, and she can both cow pony and pack. Jumping fences at will for greener pastures, she has the admiration of all the cowboys for her personality and willingness to work.

segment of the state receives its water from the Sierra and depends on its rainshed. It is a very important range.

In beginning this book I metaphorically cast a stone into the mainstream of cowboy culture and followed the ripples to where they led me. My car had broken down, and I thought myself stranded in Lone Pine, California. Then I met Pat Farlander of the local chamber of commerce, and in short order she had me in touch with 1,000 whooping cowboys and the Monache Old-Timer's Rodeo. It was here that the book was started in earnest. And it was here that I met John Lacey of the Double Circle L who proved to be like a brother to me, taking me along with his cowboys (the finest bunch of buckaroos you'd ever want to meet) and playing host at Christmas time for his annual crab feed. He passed me along to other ranchers like Richard Rudnick of the Onyx Ranch and Buck Elton and Bill Thornburgh of the Cabin Bar Ranch. I had many fine meals in the warmth of Bill's home with his family Tracie, Callie, and Joyce. I spent time on the Samontaguma Ranch with Scott Kemp and his wife and his dad Sandy. Cowboy Leaky Oliva and his wife Ethel treated me well and told me much of the cowboy history of the area. And the damndest cowboy town of them all was Likely, California, in the most northern portion of the area covered in this book. It's called Likely because you're most likely to meet a Flournoy within five minutes of being in town. It's true! I wandered into the Most Likely Cafe where Pearce Flournoy was eating lunch and for the next three weeks traveled the million acres of the family holdings.

This book has given me the happiest two years of my life, and I would like to acknowledge all those singularly unselfish people who gave their time in helping me put it together; to Dale Ogar, who transcribed tens of thousands of spoken words. Her astonishing technique made the words come to life and saved us an entire drafting. Clare Bell and Doug Mullen's wife, Debbie, both helped with the first oral histories. Gary Thorp gets an extra big thanks for his editorial assistance. His extraordinary skill in editing all the volumes of oral histories into a readable and entertaining work makes the cowboys' stories come to life. His constant good sense of humor and love for the western ways were welcome ingredients. My gratitude also goes to an enduring friend, Charles Kemper, whose darkroom and studio I used over the entire two-year period. Also to the men at Gamma Photo, Jerry and Peter. Especially I am grateful to the people at Northland Press, in particular to Nancy Solomon, my editor, whose high spirits and knowledge of the book business made our sessions together both creative and enjoyable. The entire book, of course, is an acknowledgment to all cowboys and especially to those of the High Sierra that I had the good fortune to meet and who gave their stories so openly. A special thank you also to Dee Brown, who has entertained and educated millions by throwing into sharp focus the human strengths and weaknesses of the early westerners and Native Americans. I am grateful for his introduction to this book but am especially grateful for his encouragement of my concept as the book was just beginning. And I cannot forget

"Big Floyd," my seventeen-hands-tall horse on loan from the Double Circle L Ranch. He had to travel twice the distance of the other cow ponies on the drives, zigging and zagging, getting me into position to photograph. And for his special ability to gallop to a knoll, turn and stand perfectly still for the exposure, and, uncanny as it may seem, walk back to the others when he heard the camera click. My appreciation to Willa Baum, head of the Oral History department at the University of California's Bancroft Library, for taking an interest in the first oral histories I had taken and, subsequently, for the introduction and acceptance of my work into the library's ten-million-volume depository. The original photographs and tapes will be kept there for future generations. I am particularly fulfilled by this.

The photographs in this book were taken with 35mm single-lens equipment using, almost exclusively, K-64 film. On horseback I travel cowboy style, very light in case the horse blows up or there's a wreck and I have to help. I take two camera bodies and both color film and black-and-white Tri-X rated at 400 ASA. I used 35mm, 105mm, and 300mm lenses. My tape recorder is a small cassette type with a lavalier mike. I have taped in every conceivable situation: in pickups bouncing over trails, in cow camps, and on trail drives on horseback with the recorder in the cowboy's saddle bag and the mike clipped under his neckerchief away from the wind.

PETER PERKINS

Introduction

For North America it began in 1521 with the arrival at Vera Cruz of six heifers and a young bull — offspring of sturdy Andalusian cattle that had been transported from Spain to Hispañola soon after Columbus "discovered" that island in 1492. Gregorio de Villalobos brought these first cattle to Mexico, and the sharp-horned, fast-footed animals thrived on the rich coastal grasslands, increasing rapidly in numbers. Long before Englishmen settled at Jamestown and Plymouth colonies, Spaniards had spread their livestock north and west, reaching Red River in 1690.

Left: At a separating corral of the Double Circle L Ranch, owner John Lacey explains: "We have a hybrid cattle, a cross between an Angus and a Hereford. Years ago the whole valley had predominantly what is called short-horned or Durham cattle. We feel that the cross puts some life into the breed and that they do better on the feed."

For three centuries the cattle adapted and evolved on the open ranges of New Spain — from Texas to California — growing heavier, their horns lengthening. When the Americans began pouring into Texas they called these cattle Longhorns, and the rangy varicolored animals made possible the development of a cattle industry in the American West during the last half of the nineteenth century. By the hundreds of thousands, Longhorns wound in trail drives from Texas to the railroad towns of Kansas, across the Northern Plains as far as Canada, and westward to the golden land of California.

Evolving along with these cattle were the men who herded them, the *vaqueros,* always on horseback. *Vaca,* the cow; *vaquero,* the cowherder. "Cowboy" came much later. On roundups and trail drives they were simply "boys," as the men in the ranks were called during the American Civil War. Kansas newspapers identified them as boys, cattle drivers, drovers, herders. Abilene was the first end-of-trail cowtown, and in 1867 its first hostelry

Above: This bull was bottle-fed from birth and is a favorite on the Flournoy Ranch.

Right: After five or six seasonal trips to the mountains, crafty cattle learn all the hiding places in the green stringers of grass fingering through the forest and are most reluctant to leave. Big John, a graduate of Cal Poly, ex-R.C.A. rodeo competitor, and now an agricultural loan officer with a bank, vacations on the Double Circle fall trail drive. "This is my idea of fun," he says smiling.

for trail drivers was called the Drover's Cottage. But by the late 1870s, "boys" became "cowboys," and Charles Goodnight noted that in order to handle a hundred thousand cattle on the famed JA Ranch, "We employed a little army of men called 'cowboys.'"

Almost everything else retained the original Spanish-Mexican flavor, at least in part: *Chaparajos* to chaps, *la reata* to lariat, *cincha* to cinch, *cuarta* to quirt, *mesteño* to mustang, *lazo* to lasso.

By the time the Mexican *vaqueros* brought Longhorns into what is now the southwestern United States, their working gear was beginning to take form. Clothing and equipment changed through the years, adjusting to climate and geography, but their basic purposes remained the same. Upon seeing cowboys at work for the first time, travelers usually described their costumes as "picturesque," but almost everything they wore and used was chosen for practicality and not for show.

Southwesterners, for instance, favored the high-crowned, wide-brimmed hats that came out of Mexico. The wide brim was needed as a shade against the blazing sun or as an umbrella against the rain or, when pulled down over the ears, as a shield against biting winds. The high crown could hold enough water to slake a horse's thirst or extinguish a camp fire. It was large enough to be used for a sleeping pillow. As ranching moved northward, however, the crowns were worn lower and flatter; narrower brims were favored, a matter of style and regional choice. An astute hatmaker of Philadelphia, John B. Stetson, made a study of the cowboys'

needs in headgear, and his product came into such demand on the western ranges that his name and the word "hat" were soon synonymous.

The early cowboys seldom wore coats while working because they hindered freedom of movement, but most wore vests because the pockets were needed to store tobacco, cigaret papers, and perhaps a rabbit's foot or other talisman. Photographs of nineteenth century cowboys almost invariably show them with their vests open. They firmly believed that buttoning a vest would bring on a bad cold.

Almost from the beginning, the American cowboy's pants were jeans, brown or striped at first, and then the blue denim of Levi Strauss, with copper rivets at the stress points. To protect their legs from cactus, underbrush, and weather, they wore chaps of many variations ranging from armor-thick leather to shaggy animal skins. Unlike cowboys in the movies, however, they seldom wore chaps when they were not at work in the saddle. On foot, chaps were burdensome, uncomfortable, and unneeded, except maybe to impress a tenderfoot or a pretty girl.

Boots equalled hats in importance. Although the wearers spent more time in the saddle than on the ground, they were exacting in their demands for shape and fit in their footwear. On range or trail, they had no time for lacing, so the boots were solid, not too loose, not too tight, the heels long so they would hold in the stirrups, but shaped so they would not become entangled in them. Attached to the boots were spurs, necessary for controlling mounts, yet used with care. More than any-thing else worn by cowboys, jingling spurs served as insignia of trade and rank.

Gloves, a pistol, and a bandana for protection against dust usually completed the ensemble. The gloves more often than not were of buckskin, with flaring cuffs deco-rated with stars, cattle brands, or fanciful geometric designs. The preferred weapon was Sam Colt's single-action revolver, designed for the Texas Rangers during the 1840s and maturing into the celebrated Peacemaker of the 1870s when trail driving was in full flower.

The procedures of the roundups — some still used to this day — were fairly well developed before the Texans started trail driving to the northern railheads. Whether they were tame or wild, Longhorns had to be rounded up, cut out for the trail drive, and corralled for branding, dehorning, and castrating.

The success of a roundup depended upon the range boss, who in the early years was the ranch owner. As big ranching developed, the owner would select an expe-rienced cowhand for the job. Roundups in the South-west began early in the spring, just before the grass was ready for grazing along the trails to the north. At the beginning of a "gather," the roundup boss would recruit about twenty cowboys, a horse wrangler to look after the mounts, and most important of all, a cook.

On range or drive, the chuckwagon was the central point, a hearth and home under the open sky. A good cook was expected to act also as blacksmith, barber, surgeon, and morale builder. As for the chuckwagon,

it was a work of utilitarian art, the invention of pioneer cattleman Charles Goodnight. The sturdy wagon was covered with canvas and equipped with a box at the rear for storing dishes, a Dutch oven, frying pan, kettle, and coffee pot. The standard staples also had their exact places: coffee, salt pork, corn meal, flour, and an abun-dance of beans. A folding leg was usually attached to the chuck box lid so that it formed a table when lowered for action. The main body of the wagon was packed with bedrolls, slickers, and extra clothing. Fastened in the front was a water barrel with a convenient spigot running through the side of the wagon.

To begin a roundup, the cowboys swept the range in all directions, searching thickets and arroyos, driving the cattle back to the main camp. There the herd was usually held in place by patrolling riders.

The next step was to separate from the herd the mature animals that were to be driven overland to market, and the calves which had to be branded for return to the range. "Cutting out" it was fittingly called, and required a well-trained pony, one that could "turn on a dime," and a rider who had a sharp eye, good mus-cular reflexes, and was an expert at handling a lariat.

As soon as an unbranded animal was roped, it was immediately dragged or herded to the nearest fire where branding irons were heated to an orange red. In Texas, all branding was done in a corral, a legal requirement devised to prevent hasty and illegal branding by rustlers on the open range. In the early years, brands were usually the initials of the owner, but a rustler could easily change

Left: "I've done so damn many things in the last 45 years, it's pitiful," Buck Bills said. He'd just gathered a dozen bulls and was saying, with typical cowboy humor, "Hell, I've known people who smelt worse and were a damn sight meaner than these Hereford bulls. They're pretty gentle — not like your Brahma — but you've got to keep your eye on any animal that weighs 1600 pounds. When I came to California in the thirties, I started with the Rudnicks in their feedlot, drivin' the mule wagon and feedin' cattle. Then I cowboyed in the Valley for a while, skinned cattle in a slaughterhouse, worked for Shell Oil, and worked for an aircraft factory on the assembly line. Finally I said to my wife, 'Let's go cowboy in the Owens Valley,' and we've been here ever since. I made the right choice."

Right: "You've got to like this kind of life, because it's tough. If I don't like a place, I'll move on. One of the nicest parts of being a cowboy is the freedom. Even if you're with a crew, you're still kind of off by yourself. It's not like being crammed into a room with a bunch of people." Skeeter

a C to an O, an F to an E, or, for example, JY into OX. Ranchers soon began designing brands that were difficult to change.

After the work of branding was completed, preparations for the long drive to market began in earnest. The routine of the roundup may have been Spanish in origin, but the technique of the nineteenth century trail drive was pure southwestern American. As early as the 1840s several long overland drives were made from Texas to New Orleans, to Illinois, and to California. Before 1834, California's Spanish rancheros and missions had almost half a million cattle, but in that year a heavy slaughter began in order to supply a growing market for hides and tallow, shipped out by sea. By the time of the gold rush, California cattle had declined to a few thousand, and the hungry miners soon consumed most of them. To supply the demand for beef, Texans drove their herds westward.

During these early overland treks, the requirements for a successful trail drive were discovered through trial and error. When the first railroads reached Kansas soon after the Civil War, to open a way to the markets of the northern cities, the southwestern cattlemen were ready with the necessary skills for moving thousands of Longhorns overland to the railroads.

Getting the average trail herd of three thousand cattle underway was almost as complicated as starting an army on a march across country. The personnel consisted of sixteen to eighteen cowboys, the cook and his chuckwagon, and the wrangler for the remuda, or horse herd. As each cowboy needed from six to eight mounts for the hard journey, the remuda usually numbered a hundred or more horses.

It was necessary to move slowly at first until the Longhorns grew accustomed to the drive's routine. After a few days, the cattle would fall into place each morning like infantrymen on parade. In the order of movement, the trail boss rode two or three miles in advance, choosing the best course and seeking watering places for noon and night camps. Behind him came the chuckwagon driven by the cook, with the wrangler and remuda off to the right or left. Then came the point of the herd, with the lead steers in front and the point riders at their sides. Strung along the widening flow of the herd were the swing and flank riders. The tail or drag riders brought up the rear, the least desirable position on the drive because they had to keep prodding the lagging cattle while they rode all day in clouds of dust and the generated heat and smells of the herd. Beginning cowboys, sometimes called waddys, were often given the drag positions.

Moving at an average speed of fifteen miles a day, some drives lasted for two or three months. It was a testing time for the younger cowboys, a time of almost

Right: Lofty clouds in endless and swiftly changing patterns can bring sudden rain in the mountain areas and coastal ranges. Here at the New Cayama Rodeo, other factors of hot sun, loose topsoil, and little vegetation to hold in moisture make it a place for only the best providers. LaMar Johnson, past president of the Cattlemen's Association, has done well here. This year he was the director of the Old-Timers' Rodeo, which collected a substantial amount of money for college scholarships for some local young cowboys.

continual weariness and danger. A violent thunderstorm or a party of beef-hungry Indians waving blankets could start a stampede in a matter of seconds, and the cry of "Stampede!" on the trail brought more terror to a cowboy's heart than any other word in the language.

But finally after weeks of dust, mud, storms, rustlers, short rations, and stampedes, most of the cattle, horses, and men survived to hear the whistle of a railroad train. At first sight of the sprawling false-fronts of the cowtown's buildings, the men lifted their hats and broke into wild yells.

> I've finished the drive and drawn my money
> Goin' into town to see my honey.

Who were these first cowboys, riding the ranges and the trails northward and westward? Most were young men in their twenties, survivors of Confederate cavalry units of a lost war, endurers of hardships, old before their time. Most had been born on the American frontier — of English and Irish and Scottish parentage — and

Left: "The banks in Lone Pine didn't open their doors one Monday in 1923. They had failed, gone broke, and my dad lost everything. Well, he had 50 cents in his pocket. It was tough, but the family held together. My brother and I worked out, day worked, 'til we had enough money to buy a pack outfit, which we ran for ten years with my dad. Then we sold that for a ranch and some cattle. We have been cowboys ever since. We're really contented with what we've got. I wouldn't change very much, looking back on it." Wilfred Partridge

although they may have been race proud, they shared their strenuous lives with Mexicans, Blacks, and occasional American Indians. One statistics-minded historian has estimated that one-seventh of the nineteenth century American cowboys were former black slaves, and another seventh were Mexicans. A few years after trail driving began, they were joined by a considerable number of young Britishers and a sprinkling of Europeans who came west in search of adventure as ranchmen and working cowboys. Many were sons of titled families, university graduates; some were black sheep in voluntary exile. They brought an exotic air to the cattle ranges.

Cowboys were first introduced to the world in popular fiction of the 1870s, but remained minor characters, in the mythology of the Old West until after Charlie Siringo published his *Texas Cow Boy* in 1885 and Frederic Remington's range country illustrations began appearing in magazines about the same time. With the publication of Owen Wister's *Virginian* (1902), a book that J. Frank Dobie called "the classic cowboy novel without cows," the myth of the cowboy was permanently established. The image of the horseman as cavalier had moved across the Old South into Texas, and then this vision of knighthood was carried northward and westward from there.

One of the undying myths is that of Cowboy vs. Indian, now so ingrained in human consciousness that it has become a child's game around the earth. Conflicts between the two certainly did occur (usually brought on by hunger because steers had replaced buffalo on the plains), but violent clashes were infrequent.

Even rarer were the dime-novel shootouts between cowboys and lawmen in the cowtowns. A thorough search of contemporary records indicates that the total number of all killings in the five major cattle towns of Kansas from 1870 through 1885 was forty-five. That was three deaths per year, fewer men than are usually slain in one Hollywood film about cowboys. What the cowboys never seemed to realize, however, was that the lawmen were in league with the gamblers and prostitutes, and that all three were interested only in peacefully separating them from the hundred dollars or so they had earned on a trail drive.

Actually, the life of a cowboy, for all its free-spiritedness, was filled with as much tedium and loneliness as afflicts the endeavors of most men. He was poorly fed, overworked, and underpaid. Yet there was something about the life that attracted a certain type of young man. "Men with the bark on," Remington described them. No other trade or occupation suited their restless, romantic, roaming spirits. Teddy Blue was sure that he would be able to recognize an old cowboy in hell, even with his hide burnt off, by the way he stood and walked and talked.

In the late twentieth century the real cowboys — like their counterparts, the American Indians — have been pushed back into the remoter regions of the country. But as this book proves, they still endure, holding on to the old ways — independent, proud, optimistic, indestructible.

DEE BROWN

Mark Dalton

Now don't fool yourself that these cows ain't dangerous!
They're nobody's pets!

THE COWBOY BELIEVES IN NATURE. There has to be something that is over everything. It could be anything. It could be the way a lot of folks explain it, but the cowboy believes it's nature that makes man and makes things happen. I've known two cowboys in my life who never spent an hour in church, but they came as close to livin' the golden rule as any men I ever knew. One had told a Catholic priest to leave his home and the other went to runnin' bars an' casinos. Neither one was religious, but they absolutely believed in doing to others as you wanted them to do to you. But most cowboys are this way. They treat the next man the way they want to be treated. But he can still go back to the old code of an

Left: "I'm still workin' at 91. I can't sit down and do nothin'. I've been a cowboy all my life. Every day there's somethin' different. When I cowboyed, we rode all kinds of horses in all kinds of weather. They picked our horses, and we either rode 'em or went lookin' for someplace else where there were gentler horses."
Mark Dalton

eye for an eye. If a man does something to him, he'll do something to that man. That makes it legal in his mind, and that's the way he lives.

A brushpopper is a cowboy that works around northern Arizona country and some of northern New Mexico. Brush country is pretty near all heavy brush. Oak brush is the only kind that don't have a hook on it. There's every kind of cactus and thorn tree. In fact every kind of thorn there is grows in northern Arizona. Well, there's runaway cattle in there. They go wild, and you couldn't drive them anywhere. The brush wouldn't let you. So a brushpopper goes in there and ropes 'em, catches 'em and ties a rope around their horns, and ties them to a tree. There are all kinds of trees in there — all mixed together — cedars and everything. Sometimes a brushpopper will tip the horns with a little coping saw so she ain't so dangerous, and then they'll leave 'er tied to that tree all night. That ol' cow will fight that tree all night to where she will halfway lead in the morning.

They call these cowboys "coyotes" because they always work in pairs. They need each other 'cause a man might get jerked down, crippled, or hurt. They try to get a cow in a small opening about 10 feet wide so they can swing their ropes to rope 'em. They can't rope 'em in brush. The next morning they'll go around gatherin'. One cowboy will have his rope around the horns to lead, and the other will follow with his rope to hold the cow back if she tries to run up and hook the cowboy's horse in front. They lead them out of the brush that way. You can't drive them out. I've seen some cowboys put a wire across the cow's horns to keep them out of the brush. It hurts 'em when they hit the brush and so they stay out. Or they'd "sideline" them. They take a rope around the cow's neck and tie up one hind foot with the other end to keep 'er from goin' back. What the cowboy is tryin' to do is to get the cattle to a pasture and hold them there 'til he can get them fattened up for market.

Now don't fool yourself that these cows ain't dangerous! They're nobody's pets! I've caught bull in that country and cow in that country that I knew were nine or ten years old, and I don't think they'd ever seen a man. If they did see a cowboy, they'd be over the next ridge right now! They won't have a mark on them, no brand or earmark. A lot of brush bulls in there will be up to fifteen years old — never been caught and never a sign of a brand on them. And I mean they are dangerous! When you start monkeyin' with those cattle, you don't know what they are going to do. I've seen 'em come at you after you roped them like they were going to eat you up. You better be ridin' a horse fast enough to get out of the way or they'll hook you for sure. Hook the horse or you or anything that gets in their way. I don't want to play around with a brush bull on the prod. When you run into one of those ol' frighten' bulls a few times, it's best to get rid of him! Make dog meat out of him!

I used dogs too, big ol' catch dogs. An ol' catch dog will catch ten cows while you're catchin' one. Those big catch dogs catch and throw. They throw anything. I've seen 'em jump in on an ol' cow over 1200 pounds and end-over-end 'er. All of them don't catch alike. Some of 'em catch on the end of the nose, on the side of the nose, or on the side of the face. They usually are pretty good size dogs. That ol' Jack dog I had weighed 70 pounds. He was a black-and-tan shepherd on one side and pit bull on the other — not the little pit bull but the big brindle pit bull. He'd bite one in the jaw and throw 'er end-over-end. After he got 'er down, for some reason or other, she won't get up. She won't try to get up. And then we'd just tie 'er. When she was tied down, we'd go to another one.

The last time I worked Babbitts' out of Flagstaff, I worked that Tonto Rim. I had two, well I actually had three dogs; I never used ol' Katty much, 'cause she was a little bit too light. She was full-blood black-and-tan with no pit bull in her. But I worked two pups and an old dog that were full-blooded brindle bull. The reason not many guys worked the full-bloods was that after the dog got the cow down he had to be pried loose. He wouldn't turn loose. A dog mixed with a black-and-tan would turn loose when I told him to.

I was workin' in Douglas, Arizona. I'd been brush-popping'. I went into Douglas, foolin' around there. My horses were in the livery stable there. This big ol' brindle bulldog took up with my horses. One day I was goin' down the street, ridin', and this big ol' bulldog was a followin' me. The Sheriff stopped me, and I wondered, "What the hell I done now?" And he says, "Does that big dog belong to you?"

And I says, "No, he don't. He took up with my horses."

He says, "You goin' to leave Douglas in the next few days?"

And I says, "Yeah."

"Well," he says, "will you take that dog with you? He wants to follow your horses."

I says, "Why? Don't he belong to somebody around here?"

He says, "We never found anyone he belongs to, and I've got orders to shoot him. I've pretty near run out of excuses for not killin' him. The only thing he's done is gettin' in the garbage barrels, and I seen him followin' your horses."

"The dog was half starved to death when he took up with my horses, and I've been feeding him for the past few days."

He says, "If you leave Douglas, take that ol' dog with you if you would."

So I said I would. I already had that ol' Casey dog. She'd quit chasing. Somebody had cowed her, and she wouldn't catch. A ol' cowboy told me she was a hell of a good catch dog at one time but she had quit. So I put these two dogs together, and that new dog was a catch dog! I mean that sonofabitch was a catch dog and a good one! And ol' Casey went back to catchin'.

In those days you paid a brushpopper by the head, not by the month. We were gettin' five and ten. That's five dollars for branded stock and ten dollars for un-branded. My wife was a brushpopper too. We worked together, and the first month we worked for Babbitt we caught over 100 head, mostly unbranded.

A year or so ago Loren Babbitt asked me if I would like to go pop brush. I told him I thought I was gettin' a little old to pop brush in that country. (He laughs at this thought.) I'll tell ya, a man never realizes it all, but when you say "brushpopper," that's your cowboy at your hardest.

Overleaf: "All the sweat and swearin' in the Sierra won't get the cattle to the top if they don't want to go. Sometimes you've just got to wait them out," says trail drivin' veteran cowboy John Lacey, owner of the Double Circle L Ranch. The long thin line of reddish brown Hereford cattle and dust-covered cowboys began at three in the morning to escape the midday heat of the desert, as John Lacey explains it, or as his foreman says with a grin, "Ol' John, he's a real early riser."

Pat Cline

Don't hit a horse! I mean, there's times
when you have to get after them
a little, but nothing heavy.

I'VE COWBOYED for just about everyone in this valley (Owens). You might say I've got the reputation of being an all-around hand, seeing how I was brought up in it. There has never been any doubt in my life as to what I wanted to do. I've always wanted to be a cowboy, even in high school during the sixties when Elvis Presley was rockin' and grindin'. I was ridin' and ropin'. When everyone else in the school had their hair all greased up ridin' around in cars goin' nowhere, I always thought they were about the dumbest bunch I'd ever seen. They were forever just "hangin' out," doin' nothin' that I could see. Of course my being a cowboy made me an outcast to most, but I've followed my lifestyle straight through to today, while most of my classmates have gone through several and some haven't found one yet.

My life has been very active, and although I've changed jobs a lot, I don't think I've been out of work for more than a day at a time. I take a lot of pride in being a cowboy and feel that I do it well. I was a lead man for the Harris Ranch — it's a feedlot with up to 100,000 head — in the San Joaquin Valley. I like working horses. It's an accomplishment and a challenge. And there are no short cuts — none that won't show up in the long run. You've got to have an understanding of horses and how they think. Same way with cows.

Since I've been married, which is eight years, we've never spent Christmas in the same place twice. We move two or three times a year and I can tell you my wife is gettin' pretty tired of it. My wife, Carol, likes Fish Lake where we are now, and I'm goin' to try to rig it so that maybe we can settle down here. Carol likes it here, and we've got a real nice place to live now. We're rentin' it, but Carol has a part-time job with a country grocery store and bar. Before we had kids (we've got two) it was okay movin' around, but it slowly got worse and worse. Now we both feel the need to settle down.

My movin' around, I guess you could blame on my temper. I've got to watch that, but it's gettin' better.

Lately I've run into some pretty non-professional employers, and I don't like workin' that way. I like workin' off a horse. My first cowboyin' job out of high school was open range brandin' for the RX Ranch that had 6,000 head. Just me and another fellow would ride the range, movin' cattle and brandin' the ones that escaped the last year's brandin'. We would come upon a yearling or maybe a two-year-old heifer with no brand. We would build a fire, and with this iron that we had rigged so it would break in the middle to carry it, we would put the old RX on her and be on our way in no time. We'd have to rope her first and tie her down, 'cause there were only two of us. At a regular brandin' you've got five people on one calf.

Right now I'm workin' on an oil rig, 'cause the money is so good. I've made as high as $3,000 in a month's time. It's a wildcat operation, no benefits or union or anything, and we all work like hell; we average about 12 hours a day, six or seven days a week. I work at the top of the rig, 70 feet in the air. I have this leather strap around my waist. When the drill comes up out of the ground, it needs an extension, and it's my job to swing out over it as it comes up and secure this 35 foot casing to it. Then I get the next one ready as they send the drill back into the ground. It's dangerous, and you have to be fast because the walls of the hole start to cave in without the casing. We change casings 80 times in four hours. The drilling collar fell in the hole Monday, and we can't get it out, so we'll have to shut down.

I've got another deal goin' with a rancher a half mile down the road from our house. It will mean some farmin' and puttin' up some hay, but they raise quarter horses and have a bunch of brood mares. I'd be takin' care of them, and I'd be in charge of the place. In the winter I'd bring in outside horses to train and breed. Also I've got a good friend who is in the race horse business who wants to send me colts to train — you know, not to race them, just to get them used to the saddle and to make sure they're cared for right. I'd have to put in more corrals and stalls, but I could get $250 a colt, and that would more than double my salary. It could work out. Carol's been tops through it all.

One time I went to northern California. I worked on an outfit, and I blew up and got mad. I had a bad habit of doin' that. I'd get mad and, boy, I'd quit. I wouldn't put up with it. I guess you could call it pride; that has been a problem with me. Carol was eight months pregnant at the time and quittin' meant we had to move. And it was rough on her. She was pretty unhappy.

I took a day off and went and got a new job. It was a good job, but it was no kind of money. But it was one of the best jobs I've ever had as far as cowboyin'. Within six months I was jigger boss, that's "lead-off man." This outfit ran 8,000 head of cattle, one of the bigger outfits. In the summertime they take 80% or 7,000 of their cattle up into the mountains in the forest, so the jigger boss takes care of them, and the cow boss stays below and takes care of all the weaners that were weaned the year before and the other cows they need down there. I lived with the crew in the forest. That was a good job as far as cowboyin' is concerned, as I said, but one of the problems with a lot of the ranches is poor management.

Left: "I've always wanted to be a cowboy. Even in high school during the sixties and when Elvis Presley was rockin' and grindin', I was ridin' and ropin'. When everyone else in the school, well, most anyway, had their hair all greased up and went ridin' around in cars goin' nowhere, I always thought they were about the dumbest bunch I'd ever seen. They were forever just hangin' out, doin' nothin' that I could see. Of course, my being a cowboy made me a outcast to most, but I've followed my lifestyle straight through to today, while most of my classmates have gone through several and some haven't found one yet."   Pat Cline

Right: "The first time we drove cattle over that 8,500 foot summit 25 years ago, this ol' buckaroo tried to do it in one day. You just don't do that. I guess he was just tryin' to test our air to see how much bottom we had. We ended up sleepin' up there on that hill behind the cattle all night long because we'd got 'em all screwed up. They weren't mothered up [cows paired with their calves]. We'd lost our leaders [seasoned cows that lead the way], and all our cows went off. We had a hundred calves in the back end; it was a real wreck. If that wasn't enough, our horses got loose, so we were afoot and finished the trip walking behind the cattle 'cause our horses went back home to the ranch."   Bill Thornburgh

They get into a bind for money, and the cowboys don't get a raise. I've had that happen a lot. The operation was a seasonal circle, driving cattle from the desert to the lakes and into the forest in the summer and then driving them out in the winter. It took ten 3-day drives to get them out of the forest. We had a chuckwagon on that outfit that made camp every night. We'd camp out by the cattle and be able to move next morning — real old-style western. I liked that.

I learned to horseshoe from my dad and his brother. It's real hard work. You're bent over all the time. It's real hard on your back. You're holding up the horse's hoof, too. I like to please the owner and shoe 'em like they say. I've been kicked lots of times. Usually the horse jerks away the foot you're holdin' and gets you off balance. Then he'll let you have it! But I can usually tell if a horse is goin' to kick by the way he acts and especially an older horse who is wise to what's happening. He'll kind of watch you all the time and try to catch you napping. You've got to stay away from them. You've got to get underneath them and hold them. If a horse won't pick up his foot for you, won't stand, tries to get away, or is always watchin' you and he snorts a lot, why watch out mister! You're goin' to get kicked! A colt is different. If you're easy with him, you're not as likely to get kicked, I've found as a rule.

Don't hit a horse! I mean, there's times when you have to get after them a little, but nothing heavy. In the long run patience is best. I got a reputation of going easy with them. I hardly ever hit a horse. Many times I don't wear spurs. A lot of times a horse will get to thinkin' about those spurs and won't concentrate on what you want from him. Sometimes an older horse will get lazy and lug a bit on you. If you want his attention to get a job done, spurs are a good way to ask him. But with a younger horse, all this is new to him. Heck, he doesn't know what's goin' on. All of a sudden here's someone tryin' to get on his back. He doesn't know that his future life is goin' to be pushing cows around and that he's supposed to go to the left when you lay the rein on the right side. By using spurs you're just adding one more worry for him.

I've got a real western background. My grandfather came across the plains in a covered wagon with his family and brothers Acey, Vacey, Pleasant, Houston, and Jim. My grandfather was a well-known veterinarian. He trained trotting horses too. He finally settled up here between Round Valley and Bishop and managed the Diablo Ranch. It was one of the big cattle ranches. That's where my dad and his brothers all grew up. He ran that ranch until the city of Los Angeles took the water down south, and all our land dried up and the lakes disappeared. I mean this valley had orchards in it, and now it's all dried up.

My grandfather had seven boys. They all had about five kids each. With most of them cowboyin' at one time or another, you can see that my family has brought a lot of cattle into the feedlots.

Right: A dry hole on the high desert section of the Onyx Ranch bakes in a setting of snow peaks and rarified air near Pacheco Pass.

Bill Carrasco

A young cowboy could be a whip-and-spur artist,
but if he won't listen, he won't make a cowman.

MY GRANDFATHER STARTED ME in cowboyin' when I was a little boy in Templeton in the Sierras. Yes, he started me by jerkin' my ears and twistin' my nose and kickin' my fanny. "Wrangle the horses, boy, and do this and do that." And that's how I started. My grandfather started in the 1860s and was considered one of the top cowmen in the Owens Valley. He cowboyed all his life. He had men who worked for him like Henry Olivas, who was a teenager when I was a little boy. He'd twist my ear too. And my uncles, Harold Gill and Wendall Gill, they taught me. But these guys would all take you in hand, and they had permission in them days to thump on you. So you did your job, and you behaved

Left: One more log and one more yarn. Cowboys, unlike the popular belief, can say a great deal more than "Yep"; they can talk all night. Almost all are versed in cowboy folklore, poetry, and unprintables. They enjoy stories on the art of cowboyin'. They speak of many things, of saddles and fences and the Civil War, of cattle and Kings Ranch, never tiring of a well-told tale.

and took the position and carried it. And if you didn't, there was somebody there to correct ya.

I was brought up to believe in a cowboy legend that the only way you could get to be a cowboy was to get through the Tunnel. This tunnel had all manner of animals in it; grizzly bears, mountain lions, wolves, coyotes, fox, and badgers. And to be a cowboy you had to go in that tunnel and get by all them animals. Each one, the way the story goes, is a friend or relative. The grizzly bears were your grandparents; the mountain lion, your parents; the wolves were your uncles; the coyotes, the cowboys; the fox was the boss; and the badgers were your friends. If your grandparents could teach you and get you passed, your folks could take over and pass you down to the uncles always snappin' at you, growlin' at you, and worryin' with you, right on down to your last job, and you could see the light at the end of the Tunnel. When you got out, your reward was being able to pick off the wall the equipment you needed for the job you excelled in. So you'd wind up being a spade-bit man, or what they call a hackamore man, or a good riata man or bronc rider, calf roper, etc. Usually a man would excel in one of these things with the help of the grizzly bears like my grandfather and old John and Albert Lubkin, Charley Domini, Russ Spainhower. They were all coyotes and fox. Friends like Bev Hunter and Roy Hunter, Mark Lacey; oh, I could name them all night. They were all badgers, keepin' you in line. You talk about snappers and biters, they were it. This is the way you have to learn to be a cowboy. You can't buy a big hat and a pair of boots and think you're a cowboy. And so the old sayin' that goes "he's been through the Tunnel" means you're talkin' about a "top hand." Now this is a secret I shouldn't be passin' on, but real cowboys know what I'm talkin' about.

There's what you call a cowman, a cowboy, and a rodeo hand. A young cowboy could be a whip-and-spur artist, but if he won't listen he won't make a cowman. The name of the game is weight an' beef an' money. You're in the business to make a living, so you handle your cattle as conservatively as you can and try to make what you can out of them and pay your bills. A lot of these boys we call whip-and-spur boys, they knock more beef off your cattle than you can put on them in a whole summer. I mean on a cow drive they won't stop and rest and make sure your cows and calves nurse and mother-up properly. So we have a problem. We have to hire them because there is a shortage of help. You have to work this kind of guy, and you have to keep one eye on him and one eye on the horse he's ridin' so

he don't spoil him. Pretty soon some of them get a repu-tation, and they can't work anywhere. They just bounce from job to job. I've done a little of that myself when I was tryin' to learn, but you should do it as a boy, when you're still learning and will respect the other man's suggestion. Today if something is suggested to them, they get mad, blow up, and quit. A young boy won't do that a lot of times, because he's been told, "Now you listen."

A cowboy is a conservative man, and he can probably do it all. He's been through the Tunnel. He's been raised on the ranch or brought up around old professional cowmen, and he's been told, "Not too much of this, not too much of that, be conservative, don't run all the fat off the cattle, save your horse, be sure that the calves are paired up with their mothers." This sort of thing. This is what makes a cowman.

A rodeo hand is an athlete, and he's damn good at what he does. Ridin' and ropin' are just the beginnin' of runnin' cattle. So a guy that goes out here for sport, why he never makes it. Now we've got what we call a "one-county tramp." That's no disgrace. He's a one-iron man. He's a boy that was raised here in Walker Basin or Owens Valley, never worked anywhere else. He never got to go over the hill and learn another ranch. My folks told me, "You go somewhere else for a while and learn another system." When you accumulate them all in one bunch, all your different experiences, you

Right: "The cook makes meals for the ranch hands and does a good many other things, too, if the occasion calls for it. She's a real good hand."   Charlie Stevensen

could usually filter out what's going to work and what ain't goin' to work. As a predicament arises you've got a better chance of makin' it work than a guy who knows just one spot.

What I'm gettin' at is this: today you get a lot of boys right off the sidewalk who buy a big hat and a pair of boots and go to the rodeo and start ropin'. The next thing you know they're tryin' to cowboy, and they'll tell you they can cowboy, and when they get out here, they foul up the whole show. They're not dependable, and they tell you they can do this and that and when they get out there, they can't. They're apt to rope a critter and break his leg or break his neck. No matter how good he is in the arena, a rodeo man might not know to pair up cattle or read brands, or he doesn't know the strays. He doesn't know ages of cattle or a pregnant cow from a dry cow. These are things that we have to be taught.

Now, Jesus, I'm not sayin' rodeo hands don't know how to cowboy! I'm sayin' *some* don't! I don't want them comin' after me sayin' I'm knockin' rodeo hands. Some of 'em are top hands. But, by God, if you want to make a livin' at runnin' cattle, you've got to come through the Tunnel!

Right: "I've got two fingers off; I put one back on, and the second one I let the dogs have." Bob Swandt, with typical cowboy humor, making light of a regrettable but unchangeable incident, goes on to explain. "If I didn't see it, I wouldn't have known it happened. I went in and heeled a steer and took a daly. The next thing I knew, the rope went out of my hand and my thumb went flying past my horse's ear. The dogs all went after it!" Texas cowboys rope "hard and fast," meaning that the rope is tied to the horn. But California cowboys like to "daly," or take turns around the horn, and they sometimes catch a finger, like two-time champion banjo picker Bob, who says, "The stub improves my pickin'."

Sandy Kemp

I guess I'm probably the highest paid cowboy in the world.

I'M NOT VERY FANCY. The corrals out there are old wood, but they are solid wood, and the cattle's not going to run them down. We've got a lot of corrals like that. They're practical and they work and that's all you need. You don't need a lot of fancy stuff, 'cause, well what's the point? Some people like nice corrals all painted white, but we never were that way. My brother and I operate the same way. We don't have nothin'. Just enough to get by. I don't have no $150 hat like some of those other guys. What's the point in having a $150 hat? This one can do the same thing as a $150 one, and the $150 one is going to get dirty just as quick if you're out doing anything. It doesn't make any difference.

Left: "A cowboy's just a person. He likes to work with horses and he likes to work with cattle and he takes pride in his job. He likes to ride the best horse and be the best roper and the best rider. He prides himself on handling cattle. You can't type him. I don't think there's any one cowboy personality. Cowboys can be fat and short and tall and jolly and sullied up and mad. You've got all kinds."

That's the way I was brought up.... San Diego County, you know, used to be big in cattle years ago. There was a world of cattle down there. Cattlemen from the old school always got by with the least they could. I was brought up with a lot of cattlemen down there. They just had enough to get by, and they always made money. You know they weren't going broke by buying a lot of fancy stuff they didn't need.

We lease all this land from the city, so that's our highest cost. We don't have anything invested in the land. On the other hand, if you own a ranch you've got to figure your investment in what you actually own. Up here you don't own anything except a few corrals and whatever improvements you want to put in. Labor is a high-cost item in this day and age. And add any equipment you've got. You need some pickups and a big truck or two and a lot of horses. We've got a hay ranch up here at Big Pine, and we've got a world of equipment just to run it, but still we don't have an excessive amount. Just enough to get the job in, and that's it. You can really save some money on the feed and grass and what-ever you can grow yourself. If we had to go out and buy that hay, it would be an additional expense. We can sell off enough hay so that it pays all the hay expenses. If you want to figure it that way, it doesn't cost any-thing. The name of the game is money, and if you're not going to make any money, get out.

Feed on the ground is good too. We've got a world of pasture. We've got pasture every place we go. That's the cheapest feed we've got. You bet. And that's the thing, you utilize your pasture in the best way you can with the kind of cattle you think will do best. I've never given much thought to what the secret is to running a good cattle business. You have to watch your costs; that's the main thing. You have no control over the market and you have no control over the weather, so if you can gear your costs to match your operation and try to make your operation efficient and if you have the right kind of cows . . . I guess what I'm trying to say is to fit your own range so that it will do the best job for you.

I don't think there's any one breed of cattle or com-bination of breeds that's really any better than any other. It's up to the individual, whatever he thinks is best. Naturally, if you think you've got a good kind of cattle that's doing a good job for you, you're going to take care of them and do the best you can with them. I've been pretty successful in coming up with a Brahma-cross. I was cross-breeding with Brahma bulls back in 1947. That's the first time I owned any Brahma bulls, and ever since then we've always had some Brahma bulls and some cross-bred Brahma cows around. As far as

I'm concerned, they're the best for our operation. We used a lot of black bulls too, and we also crossed the Brahma bulls with the black cattle. The cross-bred Brahma cattle have very little pinkeye and very little hoof rot. The Brahmas raise a heavier calf than the straight Angus and straight Hereford cattle we've had, and we can sell them for the same price that we get for the Hereford or Angus. We're not discriminated against because they're half Brahma or quarter Brahma or what-ever. We get the same amount of money per pound as the other cattle, and the buyers seem to like them.

We had a ranch in San Diego County that we sold last year. It was on the desert, and it was a straight desert ranch. I mean everything down there had a thorn on it. There were cholla and barrel cactus and cat claw and mesquite and ocotillo. It'd get up to 120° in the summertime down there. But the Brahma cattle were the only kind of cattle that would live down there. The Herefords just couldn't stand the heat. They lived, but they couldn't do any good. Of course we don't have the extreme heat up here, but the Brahma cattle can also stand the cold. Maybe they couldn't stand it in Mon-tana or Wyoming, but it doesn't seem to bother them up here. They get along real good in the wintertime.

And the Brahmas don't have the flies. Flies'll get on a Brahma but not as bad as they do the other cattle. The Brahmas got a sweat gland, and they give off an odor. They kind of smell like a goat if they get real hot. And maybe the flies don't like that.

One of the most expensive parts of the cattle business is the cowboy. I guess I'm probably the highest paid cowboy in the world. I do like to cowboy. I've cowboyed all my life. I mean that's all I've ever done. I've spent more time on horseback than anything else I guess. I haven't spent as much time in the last four or five years, because I've been trying to get these ranches straightened out and settled up. But I rode a lot of horses all my life. That was the only tool we had to work with — a horse. I started riding when I was eight or nine, something like that, and you just didn't do anything else.

That's another thing about the cattle business. There's a lot of romance to it, and that's probably the greatest thing that's wrong with it. You get a lot of people in the cattle business that are going into it just for the romance. I mean they want all the romance, and they want to wear a big hat and they want to parade around as a cattleman or a cowboy or whatever. A lot of times that's not too good, because you get these people in here doing that sort of thing. Well, they run the price of cattle up. They run the price of ranches up. And it gets all out of perspective. Of course that's something you can't do anything about, because this cattle business has always been a romantic business. Frankly, I fail to see where the romance comes in, but that's what they tell me. It must be, because every damn fool I know wants to own a cattle ranch or be a cowboy or something.

I don't think there's been an awful lot of changes. The ranches themselves are changed. They've become smaller. But the biggest difference I've seen is that years ago they didn't have the horse trailers and stock trucks as much as they do now. When I was a kid growing up in San Diego County I didn't know of anybody who

had a horse trailer. If you were going to go somewhere, why, you just got on the horse and you rode. They had cars and trucks, but people just hadn't gotten in the habit of using horse trailers. When I was growing up, they didn't have to drive the cattle to slaughterhouse like they did 60 years ago. They trucked them, but the trucks were a bit smaller. We used to get 29 head of steers on a truck. Today they'll put 50 or 60 big steers on a truck.

We start to brand calves in the spring. We drag all of the calves to the fire. We corral them and rope them and drag them up to the fire. Of course a lot of guys are using a calf chute, so they don't have to rope the calves anymore. There again, that's a matter of opinion. I think it's faster to do it the way we do it. That's why we do it. It's also a lot more fun. These boys get a bang out of catching these calves. If we went to a calf chute, which I don't intend doing, I don't think those boys would quit, but I think they'd get a little salted up. Like I say, I think we can do it as fast or faster than they can with a calf chute. It's just as easy as far as I can see.

I don't think there's any one personality of a cowboy. Cowboys can be fat and thin and short and tall and jolly and sullied up and mad. What's the personality of an attorney? You've got all kinds, and a cowboy's no different. A cowboy's just a person. He likes to work with horses and he likes to work with cattle and he takes pride in his job. He likes to ride the best horse and be the best roper and the best rider. He prides himself on handling cattle. Well, just like anybody in any other profession, you can't type him. We've had all kinds working for us — good ones, bad ones, and indifferent

ones. I've seen a lot of them come and go, but they do take pride in their work. I've never had one bitch or complain about the long hours. They'll get tired and they'll get mad, but they won't say, "Goddammit I don't like this job, it's too damn hard, we're working too many hours and we don't have any time off." I've never had one do that. You've got to get up at 4:00 in the morning and go until 4:00 the next morning, if that's what the job takes. Everyone I've had working for me just does it.

Of course these guys are working steady for us. They work the year 'round. There are certain times of the year when there's not a lot to do. They might work four or five hours in the morning, and then if they want to, take some time off in the afternoon. If they don't have anything to do, they can go down to the bar or go home and talk to their wives or whatever. It evens out. I don't care if they drink, as long as they don't come to work in the morning drunk. They can go out and drink all night if they want, and I don't give a damn. That's their business. As long as they can get up in the morning and catch their horses and get on 'em without falling off and do a day's work, why, who am I to tell them not to drink? I drink a little myself. But I have fired a couple of guys for coming to work in the morning drunk.

Left: "What I like most about cowboyin' is that each day there is something different to do. It's not the same old factory routine every day. You hear that from most cowboys," says the cow boss Jug Perez. "There's always so much to do. Each day I've got to decide what's most important for me and my men to do — brand, ship cattle, spread salt, or gather cattle."

When the guy got to the corral and he was drunk and I could see he wasn't going to do any good, I told him to roll his bed. That was all. There's no point in putting up with that. That probably wasn't the first time he'd done it, you see. If a cowboy has a problem with his drinking then I have to fire him.

I've discharged others because they came to me and said, "I'm a cowboy." We give them a couple of horses to ride and whatever they're going to work with. I can tell in the first 30 minutes when a man's horseback if he's a cowboy. I've discharged quite a few of them, because they weren't cowboys and I couldn't use them and that wasn't anybody's fault. They thought they were cowboys. A lot of people think they're cowboys, because they can ride a horse a little bit and wear a big hat and a pair of boots. But that's not quite the case. You can tell if a man knows what he's doing by the way he works around a herd of cattle or the way he's handling his horse. I don't think anybody ever fooled me. Most of these guys say they've worked on the biggest ranches in the world and done all these things. Some of them I've kept on because I could get by with them. I could find a place for them. They could work on the ground and they weren't too much in the way on horseback; there was always some good hand covering up for them, so I've let it go. These guys are pretty good. They might like some old kid. We've had guys come that were nice people, and they got along, even if they weren't much as cowboys; we'd kind of let it ride. But I'd watch the other guys. They were backing this old boy up, because they knew a cow was going to get by him, and they'd

Above: "We don't carry water on these desert drives, 'cause if we start drinking it in the middle of the day, we can't stop. We never can get filled. So we get our fill in the morning and at night when we get to the watering holes like China Garden and Crystal Springs where we camp. We maintain these watering holes, and the cattle know where they are. If you get them halfway to one, they'll never turn back on you; it gets to be 120° out here."   Bill Thornburgh

Left: A High Sierra cowboy is silhouetted against the range of light, the massive wall of the Sierra Nevada, 55 miles long and rising as high as 14,494 feet. This awesome escarpment was created partly by the uplift of the Sierra block and partly by the down-dropping of Owens Valley. Buck Bills scans the lofty high desert plains in search of bulls to relocate on land with non-grazed feed.

cover up for him and turn it back before he made a boner. They'd ride in front of him or something.

Here I'm running an outfit and I'm the boss, but these guys are working for me and I've got to figure that they've got shortcomings and they've got things they can do good, too. You can't run over them rough-shod and cuss them out and get mad at them. There's an old saying that only a fool can't get mad, and only a fool shows he's mad. Sure, you can get mad, and these guys will blow up and they might sulk and they might quit or whatever. As long as they're doing the best they can, why, you work with them and put each guy where he's going to do the best job for you. That's all. You can drink with them and be friends with them and all that, but you don't have to be overbearing. I've got one guy up here who's worked for me 16 years, and I've got several of them who have worked 4 or 5 years. I've had to let cowboys go after they worked for me 10 or 15 years. I fired them because they had problems. Sometimes it's a personality problem — they can't get along with the other cowboys. Even if they're damn good men and very good employees, if they can't get along they've got to go. I have put up with an awful lot from cowboys with their various problems, but by the same token they have done a good job and were honest men. It's just like an old horse. I've had some old horses that were the dirtiest, rotten damned old things in the world. They'd kick at you and were hard to saddle. You couldn't catch them and they'd try to buck you off. But when you got in the middle of that old horse and you really had to get something done, he'd damn sure wouldn't let you down.

He'd get the job done. As long as he could do the job, why, you could put up with that kind of stuff. And it's the same with a cowboy. They got bad faults, but as long as they can get the job done, you have to overlook the faults, because you're never going to get all your squirrels up one tree anyway.

I like the cowboys. If I didn't like the cowboy, I'd be in a hell of a shape. I can't do it by myself. I've got to have 'em. I've cowboyed and I know what it is and I think that's pretty much true of any rancher. I can go out and work with these cowboys. Yesterday I was with them, and today we're going to work a bunch of cattle up here.

I'm the boss and, shit, I can write my own ticket. I can do anything I want to do, but I don't think you can run a cattle ranch from a desk, and you can't run it from the front porch. You've got to be with the cattle and the guys that are working with the cattle. Sure, I've got a lot of book work. I write all the checks, and I raise the financing and the whole ball of wax. I do the buying and the selling, but that's what you call a manager's job. That still isn't a full-time job.

There *is* a little difference in the professionalism of the cowboys between the 1930s and now. I think the ones years ago were a little more conscientious in a way. I think they had a little more expertise in handling cattle. That's not anything against the ones today, because those old ones grew up in a different time and a different environment. The problem today with the cowboy is that there are too many distracting things for him to do. There's more rodeos today that he can go to. And he can get around better in transportation and cars. Years ago the cowboys came up here, and they didn't have anything else to do. They were a little different breed. But I'm not saying that, under the circumstances, they wouldn't be like the guys are today. They just never had the opportunity. Rodeo has had a definite effect on cowboys. A lot of them get pretty good at rodeoing; why, they can ride a bucking horse or rope a calf rather than get a job. And there have been cases where a good cowboy quits a ranch job and takes another job, so he can rodeo on weekends. Years ago we didn't have that type.

Many cowboys comment on the continuity and closeness of their lifestyle to nature and how their work and prosperity revolve around a cycle that they both understand and enjoy. The sun shines brilliantly in the clear mountain sky as the cowboys head out to make a great circle that will encompass over 25 miles in their search for cattle. Traveling light, they carry no food, but only a slicker as precaution against sudden Sierra storms.

Scott Kemp

Cowboys are more gentlemanly than ordinary people are,
and they are very careful about how
they speak and act when a woman's around.

THERE'S LOTS OF OVERTIME in the cattle business.
We ship cattle in the spring and in the fall. We're shipping them in the spring up to Crowley Lake, and in
the fall we drive them down from Crowley Lake to
Bishop, where they're pregnancy tested. Then we ship
them to Lone Pine and Big Pine. Sometimes, if we only
have one or two trucks, we'll be loading cattle 'til 10:00,
11:00 at night. But in between, you go down to the bar
in Bishop and have a couple of rounds and then go back
and load the cattle up. There's a lot of stories about those
times. We were shipping one night, and we loaded at
about 7:00. We had another load to ship. It was just going
to Big Pine, and the truck got back up there at Bishop
about 9:30. Well, in the meantime, from 7:00 to 9:30
we were down in The Embers in Bishop. We'd had a
few drinks. It was Danny and Ronnie and I that were
loading the truck. We all got back to the corrals, and
we'd just wait in the truck for the cattle truck to get
there. So we were waiting there, and Danny falls asleep.

The truck comes, and we couldn't wake him up. There
wasn't anything we could do to wake him up. So Ronnie
and I loaded the truck. We had a little bit of trouble
loading it. Danny never woke up. He didn't wake up
until the next morning. I don't know what he drank,
but it sure hit him, whatever it was.

I think the main reason that the old-timers think
that cowboys today aren't really cowboys is that the old-
timers aren't able to do what they used to do as well.
If they see a guy that has a halfway decent reputation,
knowing cattle a little bit and being able to rope and
handle himself with cattle, they'd like to be like that
again. I think they're just a little bit jealous. I think one
of the main reasons that we don't rope around my father
too much is because he was a hell of a roper, one of the
best in the country; but he's not anymore and that bothers
him. He's not as agile on a horse as he used to be and
that bothers him, too. So there's no showing off. I've told
this to 'most everybody, and they understand what he

was, too. A lot of these guys that were good resent getting old a little bit. They did a lot of things when they were young and things might have been a little rougher. They probably went on longer cattle drives, and they did things a little bit different. But there are still cowboys today. And there's still good ones.

The cowboys today like to get in the arena a little more; they like to win a little money roping and bull-dogging, whatever they do, bronc busting. A lot of the older cowboys didn't get a chance to do that as much. They might resent that a little bit.

I talk about it every once in a while with a rodeo cowboy. I don't think they're cowboys. They don't know anything about cows; I mean 95% of them don't. They've never even seen a cow, except a steer, and those things aren't cattle. They're not a commodity for the American market. All they're for is to run down the arena for somebody to rope. Some of them are seven, eight years old, and they only weigh 450, 500 pounds. They're not fed right. If they run good, they'll keep them. If they stop running, then they go for hamburger.

A bunch of guys get together at a place like the Monache Rodeo. I thought that was a good thing. There were a lot of cowboys there, and there were a few people who weren't cowboys too that participated. And that's fine, too.

But the word *cowboy* is just used too broadly. In my opinion, a cowboy's a guy who knows cows. And these rodeo people aren't cowboys. More and more they come from universities. Cal Poly has a fantastic rodeo team, and there are several other colleges that do too around

Arizona, New Mexico. I really don't follow it at all. I know who Tom Ferguson is, and that's about as far as it goes. I don't think I could name another one, and I don't think that my father would even know who Tom Ferguson is. If he did, it would surprise me. He might know Larry Mahan or Jim Shoulders, some of those older guys.

I guess you could say my position with the ranch is foreman. I'm second-in-command when it comes to who works and getting the guys lined out. My dad doesn't tell them anymore where to go or what to do. I think he just got tired of doing that. He'll tell me that we're going to go to such and such a place and to get everybody lined out. He'll call up Ronnie once in a while, if he wants to send us different places or something. I pretty much tell guys what to do during the work. I make some of the decisions. But I don't decide to do something without first talking to my dad.

This outfit's pretty big. I don't know what the exact acreage is, and I don't want to say for sure because I don't really know for sure. We have two people employed now at Lone Pine and two here in Independence. In Big Pine, that's the hay operation, there's three people employed, and then there's one guy in Bishop. And then, of course, my father. The man in Big Pine has been working for the ranch for 15 years, I guess, Dink Martin. He runs the hay operation up there, and he's a good man.

After college, I came back here to learn to be a cowboy like everybody else. At first I was tough, because I was a college-educated, $10,000 screw-up and I used big

Above: "I've got the only all-girl crew in the Sierra — that's how my friends like to kid me, anyway. My daughters can handle all the jobs on the ranch the same as any cowboy. Our ranch is a family operation, a way of life." *Bill Thornburgh*

Right: "I'm 25 years old, and I've been cowboyin' for 20 years. All the way through high school I knew I was going to be a full-time cowboy. I'm running the family ranch now, and I'll keep doing it 'til there's no such thing as a cow, or until the government taxes us out of existence." *Pearce Flournoy*

words and a lot of these guys didn't understand that and they kind of resented me a little bit. Jug, for one, thought I was after his job, and he was going to lose his job. I had long talks with Jug, and I said, "I want you around here. I want to get along with you, and we'll go do whatever we have to do to get along." We finally got along real well. But it was tough for a while, coming back I knew I was the boss's son and everybody thought that I expected to be put in a position of running an outfit or telling people what to do immediately because I was the boss's son. I didn't want anybody to think that I was going to do that. I've been accepted by everybody now and pretty much respected, I think.

My father and I have never had the best communication in the world. Sometimes we get in pretty good arguments. But other times we hardly even talk, and everything seems kind of understood. He has tremendous responsibility for these ranches, and ranches in San Diego County. He's put this whole thing together by himself. I think, more than anything in the world, he wants somebody to respect that, and I don't know if he feels that anybody does. He doesn't know how to tell me that I do a good job, and I don't know how to tell him that he's done a good job, so we're kind of stymied. But he has got a lot of respect from every rancher in this valley. Anyway, it's been a good life.

I don't know where I want to go from here. I would like to run a ranch completely. I think I could do it. I've always felt that I could leave here and go somewhere and be able to convince an owner to let me run the outfit. I've always felt that I could be doing that now,

if I wasn't here. I like that feeling! Yeah! That's my profession, my life! Most of the magazines I get are livestock and farm journals. There's so much to a ranch.

One of the things I haven't even touched on is probably the most important thing in the whole ranch — irrigating. That's it. If you get that grass to grow, you're doing something. I go out with my dad, and we survey ditches all the time; we're always putting in ditches. I run the Cat, a job I hate, but I do it. And we're running a tractor. Danny and I were running the Cat and tractor between here and Lone Pine for almost a month. We had breakdown after breakdown, but we'd get as much done as we could. It seems as if we're always building water boxes and putting in new ditches and spreading water. That's my job most of the summers — to irrigate this whole end of the valley. Danny and I can repair most of the breakdowns. All I have to do is look at a book to see what it is. We do most of the work. I put in new bearings on the Cat last summer and replaced the radiator. Something was wrong inside the fan belt, and I fixed a piece in there. There's all kinds of equipment problems. Every once in a while something comes up that I don't know anything about. I have a friend who works as the main Cat man for the county. I call him out on a Sunday and give him a quarter of a beef and make him work all day. That works out pretty good.

The biggest thing in making the ranch go is the market. We're a cow-calf operation. We do buy and sell a few steers, but the main thing is the market. If you've got a good market, you're going to make money. And this last year was a good one. But some years, you know,

"I made over $20,000 in the mines with less knowledge about it than I know about cowboyin', where I can only make $8,000. But there's no question in my mind about a choice — cowboyin' is a good life. When I'm workin' with a guy like Jug, why, it's down-right pleasurable, even though he can get a bit ornery once in a while. We've got this runnin' bet — a six pack on every clean ropin' [with the loop around only the horns]. It makes it fun." Kenny

it gets pretty tight, and we don't buy too much. We put together a lot of things that we just have around.

Then, of course, if we get a good year, we've almost got to go out and buy a lot of stuff — we've got to spend the money somewhere. We can amortize some of it. But when we get in a lot of money at once, we've got to have a lot of ranch expenses that we can write off somewhere.

I've never had any complaint about anything I've ever bought as far as equipment or anything. My father-in-law's in the hardware business, and he's a top man in the business. He has a big hardware store down in Santa Ana. His basic philosophy is to have it — if somebody needs a part — to have it. It doesn't matter how much it costs. If you need it now and it's there, you'll pay for it. That's his philosophy, and he's got more stuff in that damn store than you've ever seen. It's an industrial supply company. Well, it works that way for us, too. I can go to a store and buy something I need today, a part for some equipment. It's far cheaper to buy the part than to order the part for half the price. What I'm getting at is that if there is something we need to do a job, then we buy it and don't worry about the price or anything else because we need it. That's been the thinking of my father. I think that's good management.

Most of the guys kind of resent having a woman here, because they like to talk about things that cowboys talk about. Cowboys are more gentlemanly than the ordinary people are, and they are very careful about how they speak and act when a woman's around. They'd just as soon not have a woman here. But we have one guy that works for us, Ronnie Bills, and his wife cooks. And when she doesn't cook, she doesn't cook! She's usually out on horseback with us.

When we go to hire somebody, we can tell within a matter of hours whether this guy is going to be a hand or not. If he performs on horseback, then he is accepted, but if not, then he's almost totally rejected by the other guys. They just don't want to have anything to do with him. We had this experience this year up at Crowley Lake. We had to go up early to mend all the fences, because we had a real heavy snow last year. And we hired this guy and he worked on the fences. He expected to go on through the works with us — the spring works. Well, everything went fine on the fence crew; he was a good worker and he was accepted. We all went out drinking and all the things that we do on Saturday night. When it came time for the works, it wasn't five minutes, he tried to get on a horse, just the act of stepping into the stirrup, and he was alienated. And he'd been pretty much accepted by everybody. Everybody thought he was a good guy. But now they didn't want to have anything to do with him. He lasted about three days, and that was it.

We sent him off somewhere else. We sent him to Big Pine to work in the hay operation up there. He couldn't handle it there either, so he went down the road. This is a tough business and maybe especially tough now when everybody is hiring minorities and women to do almost any kind of man's work.

You know, I'll get eight or nine phone calls every year from people wanting to work and just coming straight out of the cities begging for jobs and taking a reduced pay. People who are making $2000 a month, they'll work for $400, just to get away, because they can't stand it anymore. Well, you take somebody that's smart and comes in, they might be able to learn this. But by the time they learn this, they get rejected by the other cowboys. The ones that make good cowboys are the kids who start when they are seven or eight years old and want to come out on a ranch and work. Usually their fathers have something to do with the ranch, or they're in high school around here, and they want to work in the summertime on a ranch. They come begging you for a job. They're the ones that make good cowboys. Some of them don't even have a high school education, but I wouldn't trade the most educated man in the whole world for a cowboy like Danny. Or there's one in town here in Independence who's breaking horses now. His name's Norman Mull. He's a good hand with cattle and he's a good hand with horses, and I'd work with him any day of the week. He and I alone could have gotten those cattle in there, because he's good if he's on a good horse. We've done it before. I can brag on these guys all day long. Ronnie's another one. I know where Ronnie's going to be. I don't have to tell him anything, ever. No kid grows up from seven years old wanting to work in the Coca-Cola factory or a paper mill. Ronnie was making $15 an hour as a dynamite man in the mine for Anaconda down in Darwin. He is working for $600 a month as a cowboy, but he wouldn't trade it. He talks about it all the time, how much money he was paid; but he wouldn't trade it for anything. Six hundred a month is pretty much standard wages to start. We hire on extra people in the spring and the fall, and we pay $550, $600 a month. Ronnie's probably making $650 or $700 now. He's got a house and meat. He can have meat every night of the week if he wants. And if they don't make too many long distance phone calls, that's paid for. And electricity's paid for, gas, everything. So it's real nice as far as that goes.

If you take 100 guys, you won't get too many cowboys out of that. I think that there's a lot more common sense to being a cowboy than there is to just learning. Some of these guys never even read a book. Some of them don't even know how to read. I don't think that not being able to read makes a person less intelligent. That doesn't have anything to do with it. Talk about somebody who doesn't know how to read, one of the typical examples of that is Jug, and he's surely not dumb. He's got a lot of cow sense. He knows how to handle cattle. He has leadership qualities, because he's big and tough and makes people listen to him.

I wouldn't say it's as difficult to become a top hand as it is to become a doctor, since they have to start so young. But these people don't necessarily study it. They experience it.

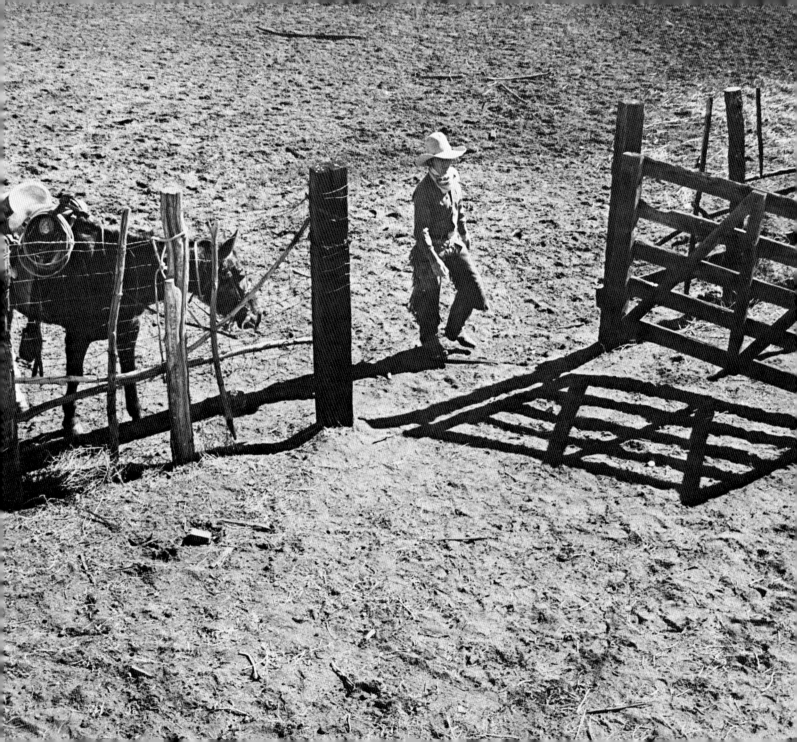

Danny Torres

Old Jug used to tell me,
"Make a hand, that's all you got to do."

I KNOW MY GREAT-GRANDFATHER was a horse thief. He got hung for it. My great-uncle got shot. He was kind of a romancer, I guess. He went messing around the wrong woman, and he got killed. My great-grandfather was born around 1830, so I imagine it happened around the '60s, 1860s, but he was a big old bearded guy. He's an old-timer, I guess. Hell, you could get away with anything just about until they finally got you.

I went to Lone Pine High. I came up here when I was about 5 years old. My uncle used to work on a ranch up here — Sierra Grande Ranch. That's how we came to this country. My uncle was the first one to come here. He's been around here for about 45 years. He's 82 years old. He's cowboyed all his life, and he's never been married. He's a confirmed bachelor, and he's been to Mexico. He spent 15, 20 years down there, because he speaks Spanish fluently. In fact, he didn't learn how to speak

Left: Danny Torres closes the last gate.

English until he was about 40 years old. He was in Mexico during the time of Pancho Villa and when they were having all that trouble along the border. He's seen a lot of it, you know, a lot of the changes from the old time.

They used to use the riatas, grass ropes, and horsehair ropes. In fact, he still uses a riata. They're made from grass. Wow, I wish I had one. I used to have one. I used to use it for calf roping. It's a good rope for calf roping, but you can't get anything too heavy. When you dally, you can't make it tight right away because it'll bust. I imagine the grass comes from the Southwest.

My uncle taught me a lot. In fact, he kind of raised me. I lived with him for 13, 14 years. I went to school

Overleaf: As soon as an unbranded animal was roped, it was immediately dragged or herded to the nearest fire where branding irons were heated to an orange red. In Texas, all branding was done in a corral, a legal requirement devised to prevent hasty and illegal branding by rustlers on the open range.

when I was living with him. I lived with him, 'cause I just liked the old man, took to him, and I just stayed with him. He's a real good old man. Usually he cooked the breakfast in the morning. We ate bacon, eggs, and lots of hot chili. Some of those old people, the Spanish, Mexican people, they were raised on chili. I love chili, too. I could eat a lot of hot chili, green, red chili. And that's what we usually ate. He was a good cook. He was mostly like a camp cook — good beans, stew, and stuff like that. Tortillas. He could make tortillas as good as any woman I've seen. Flour and corn tortillas. He does it by hand. He's good. He taught me a lot.

We didn't have electric power. We had one butane light, and the rest were kerosene. We'd have to heat the water to wash up. No shower or nothing like that. We took a bath in a tub; you know, we'd heat the water and pour it in and take a bath.

During the summer I worked at pack outfits and hay ranches. In fact, I used to work for Lacey's too, part-time in the summer. The first time I was ever in the mountains, I was five years old, with my dad. It was a pack trip. We used to do that every summer. We had a couple of pack horses. We'd help the guys drive cattle up there, too, kind of like for pleasure.

Maybe someday I'll get a little place or lease some land and run a few head. That's what I'd like to do eventually. A while back you could work for an outfit all your life and still make six-and-a-half a month and a house and some meat and utilities. But nowadays it's so hard to get started. Guys who want to get into the cattle business, and buy some land or something, maybe

get 50, 60 head. It's harder than hell unless you can get a hell of a loan and have a lot of people to back you up. If I were going to do it, I don't think it would be in this country. You could go up north and get a pretty good, small place with a little bit of winter feed and pretty good summer feed. Or maybe Nevada, but Nevada is so dang cold! Some of that country is pretty good country. The best place, I think, would be New Mexico, Arizona, down in there. It's just hard to get a place like that. The land is so danged high now. Cattle are so high. If I could get a contract with steers, lease some land, and get some good desert land, I'd stick them on there and just get the gain on them. To get started, I really don't know how I would do it. It just depends on what kind of luck you get, the right people to know.

I'm a hand, a top hand, I guess. Right now I'm working for Scott. He's up here every year. This is his job, running the calves and the heifers out. He's the cow boss of the outfit. We run about 6000 head of mother cows, and we get quite a few steers too — usually about 1500 or so, mostly crossbred cattle.

My job is to work the cattle. When we're branding, I need a little help. I think branding's a lot of fun. That's the best time of the year, because you're doing a lot on

Right: The old-timers used to say that if you've done a good day's work, you don't have to pay no mind to nobody, but you damn sure better laugh at the cook's jokes. Coffee is the favorite in the cow camps. It is made by adding grounds to cold water and an eggshell. The coffee is removed from the fire when it is short of boiling and the grounds are settled with a cup of cold water. In the morning before sunrise you can hear the cook shout, "Coffee's on the stove — feet on the floor!"

horseback. I'd rather be on horseback than behind a shovel any day. Spring, that's the best time, because they're gathering a lot of cattle. You're working all the time, seven days a week. You don't get any triple time for working on Sundays. You get three square meals a day and your regular pay, and that's about it. Scott hires a cook. We'll pull a chuckwagon, kind of like a wagon train. We just move. We usually start down at Little Lake. And we gather and ship all those cows out of there up to Long Valley. We truck them. It's probably over 100 miles up the valley. We'll put them off in a field by Lacey's and we'll brand them. We'll usually brand them a month before we go to the mountains; that way they'll have time to recuperate. We'll put them out in that feed, and they'll be in good shape when they go to the mountains. We vaccinate calves for black plague and cuprate. We vaccinate the cows for anthrax and cuprate, and sometimes we get the calves, too. We used to vaccinate the calves for anthrax. We don't anymore, though. Sometimes we'll give them vitamins for A and D deficiency. We just brand everything and move up to George's Creek. That's where they summer.

We used to brand everything down here and then ship them. Now we ship everything up there, and then we just go right up to Big Pine or Bishop. We stay up there about a week and a half, just solid, branding every day and working cattle. You fell all the calves and drag them to the fire. We usually have three or four ropers, and everybody takes turns. Everybody works on the ground. Everybody ropes, so we don't have guys who can't rope. You've got to be able to do everything.

It's a lot of fun, you know. It's a good workout. You work your butt off, but you eat good, too. Then we go out and party all night. Have a good time at night. Hit the bars. All of the guys are married. We're all about the same age. We all grew up in the same area and knew each other. We get along good, you know. We've worked around each other quite a bit. We work pretty good together, and all of us are pretty well organized. Everybody on this outfit's usually hired. The old man doesn't like any free help or nothing. He wants everybody hired. That way we seem to work better together, and we don't get a lot of these weekenders that just want to put on a rope or two or put a brand in and that's about it.

I've been through a lot of cold and hot and long days. Probably one of the longest days was up at Long Valley. We were shipping cattle. A couple of our trucks broke down, and we shipped all around the clock. We shipped all night, and it was cold, just miserable. And, Jesus, you'd have to get right in the chute with those calves and push them up that chute. They're hell to load. The next day we had to gather some first calf heifers. Hell,

Right: "Only a cowboy or a crazy person would be out in that kind of weather. The snowflakes were the size of walnuts, and that cold wind was cuttin' right through our Levi jackets. The truck we were haulin' our cattle in went onto the muddy shoulder and overturned, trappin' most of the cattle. We torched a hole in the top and got most out. We only lost two head, but our best bull took off. I don't know where he thought he was goin', but I guess he didn't want any more truckin', 'cause he was long gone. We finally caught him when his feet got sore from runnin', but he led us on a good chase in the snow first." Jim Vanloan

"*The Laceys taught me how to cowboy. I was a green kid up from Los Angeles. My folks came here when I was nine, and I was plenty scared. I thought there were Indian wars and scalpin's goin' on in the Owens Valley. From what I can see on the TV, it looks like they're tryin' to keep that myth alive in the minds of kids today.*" Tom Fogarty

it started snowing! We were gathering them in about six, eight, ten inches of snow. Boy, it was miserable! There was an old shack there where we had to wait for trucks, and we sat in this old shack drinking. All we had was coffee. We didn't even have whiskey. This old shack didn't have heat, and we were just freezing. Some of us just sat in our pickups. That's about the most miserable day, I guess.

I rode broncs up at Monache Rodeo. Once I won two firsts and two seconds. They didn't have an all-around. I don't know if I would have won it or not. That was a hell of a rodeo. I really enjoyed myself. Bareback or bull riding is probably my best event. There are rules. For bareback horse riding, you've got to start in a chute. You've got a riggin' with a handhold in it. You stick your feet out, and you've got to start the horse out of the chute. You have your spurs in him over the point of his shoulders when you come out, until the first jump. Then you mark the spurs over his shoulders with your feet and just fall back with your feet in front of you every time he bucks. And you can't touch anything with the other hand. It requires a lot of balance and arm strength. You get a big old stout horse, and boy, you feel everything. You're right in the middle of him. You know when he hits the ground. He can go either way, and it just jars you every time.

I used to rodeo quite a bit in high school when I was younger. I've been at it about 11, 12 years. I'm 24 now. We used to have rodeo teams — high school rodeo teams — and we used to travel all over the place. So we were doing it pretty regular and had a league, just like basketball and football. Every school had a rodeo team. We'd have rodeos at Bishop, Lone Pine, Lancaster, and on down the line. I wouldn't say I'm a professional. I'm just trying to make a hand, that's all.

Old Jug used to tell me, "Make a hand, that's all you got to do." He's a hell of a hand, that guy. I enjoy it, and it's a good living. I'd rather be doing this than sitting behind a desk making twice as much as I'm making now. I don't believe in that. I've never tried it. I never have had any kind of job like that. I've packed and worked on hay ranches and cowboyed and been around mechanics. My dad was a mechanic. I've learned a little bit about welding and driving trucks. I drive a truck a lot for this outfit, hauling cattle. It's just a little bobtail. We haul about 12, 13 head of cows in it, and that's about it. We make a lot of short loads.

I've been injured lots of times. I've been kicked in the head and pawed in the head. I've never busted a bone, but I've been kicked quite a few times. One time I got knocked out. I was by myself. I was down in the desert last year. I was alone out on a camp, mostly taking care of water and cattle. I had a horse, and I was trimming his feet. Somehow I stepped into him, and he kind of cow-kicked. You know, he reached forward and hit me on the head with his hind foot — just knocked me under him, knocked me out. And then he just stepped on me, smashed my whole leg. My leg was swelled up, but I was knocked out, probably about 15, 20 minutes. It was my own personal horse. Belongs to me, I raised him since he was a year and a half old. He's gentle, you know, but I was just in the wrong position and he got me. I

Winter Desert Drive

I rope mountain lion an' grizzly bear,
I use cholla cactus fer combin' my hair.
I cross the dry desert, no water between,
I rode through Death Valley without no canteen.
At ridin' dry desert I'm hard to outdo;
I'm a high-lopin' cowboy an' a wild buckaroo.

This was written by a cowboy who lived in Big Pine and
worked in the Sierra — Curley W. Fletcher.

Right: "Don't let 'em back — don't let 'em come back.
Drive them cattle up!" the cow boss was shouting, but back
the cattle came. It was too hot. The cattle were thirsty and
they knew water was down the mountain, so the cowboys
had a wreck on their hands. Cows called their calves and
bulls bellowed while the trail driver, like a nomadic tribes-
man following the weather, headed for the greener pas-
tures of the High Sierra. Tired, hot, and thirsty calves
wanted to go back to the last watering hole, while tired,
hot, and thirsty cowboys wanted the next watering hole.
This trip it was cattle, one; cowboys, zero.

get angry at that sort of thing sometimes. But I try to hold my temper.

You can't lose your temper every time a horse does something wrong with you. I've seen guys get mad at them, beat them a little bit, and that's the wrong thing. You've got to have patience with a young horse. I don't like to take things out on an animal. Sometimes I do, but I think everybody that's worked around them does.

I don't like a real big horse, just a pretty good traveling horse that you can do just about anything on. I like to start them myself. I like to ride young horses. Everybody rides a few colts. I like a Snake Fork Saddle A-frame, slick fork, and a high cantle. A four-inch cantle. I just got a new saddle this year. I had it made up in Bishop. Brad Whitman made it, and it has a four-inch dallyhorn and bucking rows. You've got to have some front end on a saddle. I think an A-frame saddle sits over all kinds. It's a good all-round saddle. You can ride all kinds of horses with different builds, like a high-withered horse and a quarter horse.

A lot of these special saddles they've got, like roping saddles, sit real low on a horse; sometimes you'll sore 'em, but we ride horses of all different kinds of builds. It's what they call an Old Mexico Tree. It's patterned after California saddles, but the old original was from those that the Mexicans developed.

I like a saddle that's light. You can get too much weight you don't need on a horse; you got a lot of strings that you can carry, you know, pack a few things with you — a coat or whatever. I like a saddle with a real free swing in the stirrups, you know, where you can get your feet out in front of you anytime. I have oxbow stirrups. I ride those all the time. They're not hard on your feet, if you're used to them. If you get a horse that blows up with you, a lot of guys have trouble. They lose their stirrups and that's it! But with these you can just turn your feet out. They're kind of narrow, and you don't want to get hung up on them, but I can keep my feet in them better than any other type of stirrup.

I've had horses go over on me lots of times. I've had horses fall down, fall over backwards, fall head over heels. I've been lucky, I tell you. I don't know if I have another sense or what. I just see it coming on, and I get out of the way. I've just been lucky.

Once I was going up to Long Valley to gather some cattle. There's some hellacious bogs up there. I mean *bad* bogs. You know that if a horse gets down in there, that's it. You're going to have to jerk 'em out with another horse. You'd be riding along, and you can't really tell where it's real boggy and where it's not. You've got to play it by ear and look where the cattle are going. Usually you know you can go where the cattle go. You follow them around.

I got in one bad spot. The horse just went down, and he panicked. He'd been in bogs before; he was a little old broke horse. I had my tie rope tucked in my belt. (A lot of times you get bucked off. You've always got to have something to hang on to so the horse doesn't get away from you. If you're out in the boonies, you'd have to walk back to camp.) But this one fell down to the left of me, and I just shot off to the right. You see, the horse tries to get out, and if you're in front of him, he'll use you to step on and get out. That's no bullshit. That's what happened. This horse, he was panicking, trying to get out of this bog. I was in his way — I was laying on the ground with one leg stuck in that bog. He was just coming toward me with his front feet. He was going to use me to get out of that bog. So I just kept on rolling. I couldn't get up on my feet, but I turned loose of that tie rope, and I just rolled away. Finally the horse just gave out. He couldn't move any more. But that was really close! Hell, he was only about two feet from me.

Other guys were about a quarter mile away. They saw I was having a little bit of trouble, so they came over and put a rope on him on the horn of the saddle and pulled him back. Just one other guy roped him. I walked over and put the rope on the horn, and we pulled him. He was kind of laying on his side and I pushed him over to where he was sitting up. He just gave up. He thought he'd had it. We were whipping on him, and he came alive. He wanted to die there, but we got him out. I still ride that horse, Cotton. I ride about five or six horses.

I call myself a ranch hand or cowboy.

Overleaf: The splendor of the Sierra Nevada is a spectacle enjoyed by the high country cowboys on their autumn drive out. In the tough terrain, they encounter varied vegetation, rock formations of granite and lava, and many rivers from the Sierra snow pack, like the South Fork of the Kern in the Inyo National Forest that the cow drive shown here is crossing.

Bob Swandt

*I crawled out in the creek an' cut that mule loose,
'cause, man, she was blowin' bubbles.*

I WAS BORN in Lancaster, Ohio. My dad was a farmer, a poor one, same as the rest of them. He was born in 1900, he was 33 when the Depression hit. I was 3. I remember when he bought a 1928 Chevrolet with a rumble seat. That beat walkin'. When it rained, it didn't make no difference. You still rode back there and hollered, "Go faster." It was tough, I guess. There was me and my sister; she's three years younger. The first house I remember was a log cabin with a wood stove. It had a front room, kitchen, and a bedroom with some dividers in it. When they moved into town, they bought a house there and kept this thing. We'd go out there in the summertime. They had some real black ground and farmed potatoes. They had a furniture shop in town. My dad ended up workin' for Ohio State University. That's where he was workin' when he died at 58. I was long gone before that.

I started to work when I was young. Didn't have TV, had to do somethin'. Wasn't many girls around there. My dad didn't drink and didn't make moonshine like everybody else. That didn't stop me from tasting it, though. Hell, when I was 10, 11 years old, I could plow and plant, cut corn, and just about anything. I've forgotten that now, though. Back then everybody worked 'cause there wasn't nothin' else to do. You didn't run to town everyday. You wanted to learn somethin'. That's what we did. When I went to bed I couldn't wait for daylight so I could get up and go do somethin' again.

I came out to California in 1962 to Shafter. I was 24 or 25, somewhere in there. I shod horses for Joe O'Brien, S. A. Kemp Stables at Shafter. They had standard bred horses. I'd had a bad back for several years, and shoein' horses was terrible on it. So that spring when they went back to Kentucky for the races, I quit an' stayed here.

When I was a kid, I was a full-fledged musician. I was as good at 10 as I was at 20. I played the banjo, the guitar, and a little of everything. Played at church. Preacher taught me to play the guitar. A guy named Reverend Clem Dennin, he started me. And my Dad sang with a gospel quartet. One of those guys played guitar, and he showed me a lot.

Then my cousin, who was nine years older, went to World War II, and he came back with a guitar player; he taught me a lot. Back in those days (I was 12, 13 years old) he started haulin' me to beer joints without my Dad an' Mom knowin' about it.

I remember old Salty. He was coughin' and hackin' one morning and buildin' a fire. I woke up . . . just didn't feel right, didn't feel like I'd been in bed very long. I looked at the watch. It was twenty after one an' he's up raisin' hell. I asked him, "What are you doin', Salty?" "Gonna make some coffee." "Hell, it's only twenty after one." "Nah, it ain't, kid." He walked over there, squinted one eye, and looked at the clock. "I'll be damned," he said, "I thought it was five after four." We made coffee, an' we stayed up the rest of the night drinkin' coffee an' talkin'. He died 'bout three years ago. He was 66 or 67. He wore those goddamned boots that if you stand up in 'em when you're drunk, you just fall over backwards.

At Brown's, they had bear bars on the windows. We'd sleep there and look out the window to watch our meat. One night Salty was layin' right there with his head too close to the window. A bear come up there, stuck his head between the bars, an' got it caught. He was pullin' backwards, just a squealin', and old Salty woke up a foot and a half from his face! He'd just opened his eyes, an' here was this bear squallin'! Boy! So he said, "I've never been so scared in all my goddamned life!"

I ran into a guy named Johnny Wilson. He was shoein' those standard bred horses, so I watched him 'bout five minutes, and I knew I didn't know anything. I got to know him and went every time I could and watched and watched. The following winter a horse stepped on his toe, and he could hardly get around. After all that time he kinda took a likin' to me and called me up. He wanted to know if I'd come help him shoe. He'd work the fire and make shoes, and I'd pull shoes, cut feet, an' nail 'em on. I did that for a few months with him and really learned a bunch. He'd make shoes for all of 'em. We'd buy the steel in eight foot lengths, measure a horse's foot, an' cut the metal and make whatever the horse wears — half round, plain plate, or whatever. The following year, Johnny quit. He told his customers to call me. So in a couple of years, I was hittin' a good lick. I was shoein' all the best stables, all the champion horses, world's champion pacer, world's champion trotter and stake horses. I had it made!

Sometimes when I'm doin' hot shoein', a person will walk right up an' pick up that shoe. They're not red hot, but you can't hold 'em. If I take a little extra long on a shoe, I'll pick both of 'em up in my hand and lay them down there. Hell, but my hand is burnt hard. A guy saw me do that one day, and he walked up, reached down there, and grabbed that shoe and ZING! Across the shop! I said, "Hot?" The smart-ass said, "No, it just don't take me long to look at a horseshoe."

Then I started racing. I asked a man to teach me and he did. Two or three days later, he started me jogging. I jogged horses all that winter, and, come March, they started training. So I learned to read a stopwatch. Luckily I hit pretty good. Come summer, he sent me to the races. We had two aged horses and two colts. Shit, I shoulda won every race, but I didn't. Experience beat me. One time I was at a fair. I had this little filly, eight years old. I was goin' on the track, and a guy ran up an' said, "You gonna win this?" "I'll try." Well, somethin' happened an' I got beat. After the second heat when I went back to the stall door with the filly, there were six or seven inches of $2 tickets stacked up in front of her stall door — to show me that the sonofabitch lost! Boy, I got so goddamned mad I started laughin'.

I got in one wreck. I was in it, but I never went down. Tommy Jefferson and I were packin'. We were crossin' one of them wet winter's creeks. The creek was five feet deep an' goin' 90 miles an hour. He was behind me, ridin', an' I was leadin' five mules. On the second mule I had my banjo, and on the third mule I had my guitar. I went across this goddamned creek, and I got up on the bank. My first mule got up on the bank, an' I had a bronco mule on the back that was still on the other side of the creek. She sat back, set the fourth mule up, and that middle mule had propane on her! Just picked her right up out of that side of the creek apullin' back. And I had my lead mules up on the bank on the other side,

pullin' back! I had a wrecker goin'. When they stretch out like that, the middle one up is just picked up and turned over. "Oh Jesus Christ!" Tom's ahollerin', "Cut my mule loose!" And I'm ahollerin', "Save my banjo!" We were across the creek ahollerin' at each other. I crawled out in the creek an' cut that mule loose (the one that was upside down) 'cause, man, she was blowin' bubbles! She went down 15, 20 yards, hit some brush, an' got right side up. Man, she just stood there. Coughin'. Damn near drowned her.

Right: Brown cow camp, with its hand-hewn pine logs, is home to cow boss Doug Mullen and cowboy Bob Swandt for the summer season. Completely isolated in mountain meadow, they will spend their days looking after the herd, each day taking wide circles into the forests of the rugged retreat. Swandt, an excellent hunter, keeps the pair well stocked with venison. Having no electricity, they must hang the meat high, away from the bears, to cool by night in the low temperatures of the mountain air and cover it by day in a corner of the cabin. Cowboy culinary finesse is reached when Doug stokes the near-century-old wood-burner range. His salsa picante is supreme. Bob is better known for remarks like "I wash my plate twice a season, once in May and once in October."

John Lacey

I think the basic philosophy is still the same —
to run a good outfit. That hasn't changed any.

I'M NOT SURE that my grandfather ever was president of the Mount Whitney Cattlemen's Association, but I know my dad was, and I was. There have been three generations in there. I took the ranch over from my father, so the Double Circle L is three generations old so far. The original brand was just a double circle. In California, in 1958, they passed a law that no two brands on the same location could be of the same configuration. They looked at them all together, and there was a double circle brand registered in another part of the state of California that was registered before our iron. It was a matter of about four days' difference in the registration

Left: "Years ago it didn't take as many cattle for people to operate. There were just more people and more land. There was a lot of land taken for the national parks: people just had a lot smaller ranches. If a guy had a couple hundred cows, that was a pretty fair deal in those days. He could make a living, but of course nowadays it's different. You have to have five times what you had in those days to do the same thing."   John Lacey

back whenever they were registered. Anyway, there were some people over in King City that had the double circle. As far as I know they still have it. My dad went over and tried to buy the brand from them, so he wouldn't have to change his. But that didn't work. But there are several double circle brands registered besides ours. The big Quien Sabe Ranch out of Hollister has a double circle registered — just the same one as ours, only it was all on the right side, rather than the left. We put an "L" on the bottom. That was what my dad thought would be the easiest way to do it, and it's been that way ever since.

I actually became active in the ranch, calling most of the shots, in 1960 when I got out of college. My dad had his first heart attack in 1943. He was fine up until about 1960, when he had another heart attack, and then he wasn't really physically able to do it all.

I was born in 1938. I was born and raised here, and I worked whenever I could. When I wasn't in school, I

Above: This cabin has a century of history of sheltering cowboys, trappers, rangers, and hikers from the changeable Sierra weather. Built by John Lacey's grandfather, its tightly chinked interior logs and earthen floor give it a frontier atmosphere.

Right: Over the years, the cowboys have established line camps to stay in overnight. Friends also put them up. It's a big night when the drive goes through the O'Leva Camp. Ethel sets a table of three meats, five vegetables, and assorted desserts. The cowboys can hear her laugh a mile off when she spots the point man. "Here come the boys," she sings, and off she'll go to set the table.

was on the ranch. Now, I didn't go to the mountains until I was nine, but anything there was to do around here whenever we were big enough to ride, you know we did it. My dad's got pictures of the first time I got on a horse. I suppose when you're three or four years old you start riding a little bit, you know, when you're just big enough so you can hang on and not get hurt.

I went to school at Cal Poly at San Luis Obispo, and I studied animal science; I just have a B.S. degree. At one time I was going to get a master's degree. I was going to go to graduate school at the University of Idaho. But about the same time, my dad was sick, and I think I probably had all the school that I could stand for a while. I also had military service that I wanted to get out of the way, so I went into the Marines and got that finished up. That's probably why I didn't finish up my education as far as any master's degree or anything. There's a lot of other things I think you gain out of college other than the animal science part. You certainly do learn some of the fundamentals that help you. Maybe not the every-day things, but you certainly learn a lot of the scientific things that could help you out. And I think that probably another very important part of it is meeting people who are in the same field you're in, who you end up doing business with the rest of your life, you know. I still meet and do business with a lot of kids that I went to school with.

Over three generations we've developed a way of running the ranch. Of course, over the years there are certain things that change an operation, whether it be the coming of the Bureau of Land Management or the coming of the Forest Service or the coming of the city of Los Angeles. I think the basic philosophy is still the same — to run a good outfit with good kinds of cattle. That hasn't changed any. This is a cow-calf operation, and it always has been. By that I mean we have cows, and each year we raise a calf crop. In earlier years when the market dictated, we kept all the calves over until they were older and raised steers until they were three or four years old, and that's how you sold your livestock. The market demanded older steers. In the mid-fifties to early sixties the market changed. We went from a steer operation to strictly a cow-calf operation where we sold the calves at weaning time each year, and we haven't varied from that since about 1958.

It's a desert-type ranch with high mountain country. There's certainly not a real steady, dependable-type climate here for feed conditions. We have a lot of variance because of the climate. We don't have steady rainfall or large amounts of rainfall, so there can be a fairly dramatic change from year to year. It makes an outfit harder to operate. We run between 1000 and 1200 cows, depending on what kind of year we have. Years ago my grandfather used to run 150 or 200 cows. It has progressed on through my dad and on up to what we have now. It kept increasing with the times, you might say, or perpetuating the ranch or building each year — trying to do something a little bit more than what we had the year before.

I definitely believe that a larger operation (maybe 2000 head) on today's standards would do better. I think our ranch here probably really needs additional summer country to summer the cattle in. We need to get into a higher elevation and get away from the valley entirely. Although modernization has helped us with vaccines and fire repellants and everything else so that we can keep cattle down here in the valley, it is still better to get them up out of the elements of the hot, dry climate into the lush green meadows. Cattle do better and the feed's better there. The calving season would start around the 15th of January and last 'til probably the 15th of June. We have a long season here because we're unable to control the bulls, so you could actually say that the first of the year is when we start having calves. The cattle are grazing, mostly taking care of themselves, through the months of January, February, and March; they're on their own. All we do is put out a little supplemental feed and see that they're tended to. That's the cycle of the winter. If the calves were all born in January, they would be three months old in the spring, but of course they're not. They're being born in that period of time, and our job is to do general ranch work and look after the cows. In the wintertime we clean up the ranch.

By the end of March we have to start thinking about putting the bulls out, getting the cattle branded and ready for the summer, and getting ready to go to the summer range. Then it's a matter of bringing them from the winter range down to the jumping-off point here at Olancha and getting them ready to go to the mountains. By June everything is branded and everything is shipped down the valley. We used to trail them down, but it's strictly a truck deal now. In June we start irrigating the meadows and spreading water. It's hay time and irri-

gating time, and the cattle are being readied for the mountains. From the 20th of June to the 1st of July, that's the time when we trail up to the summer country. We have to go up there, take care of them in the summer and fix fence and spread salt and take general care of the cattle. Of course, there always has to be somebody in the valley taking care of the cattle here, and it's the same procedure as it would be in the mountains.

Then in the fall of the year, we're gathering the cattle, bringing them out, and getting them ready to sell and ship to market. That's the time we wean the calves and save the heifer calves to put back in the bunch and clean up the cows. We sell all the old cows and the dry cows and keep our bunch cleaned up to continue our operation. Generally we always gather here at the ranch by the first of October. And generally all the calves are shipped someplace by the first of November. The cows that are left are all trailed back up to the winter range, and the cycle starts over again.

We have a hybrid cattle, a cross between an Angus and a Hereford. Years ago the whole valley had predominantly what they call short-horned or Durham cattle. From then on, each rancher, according to his preference, started bringing in a lot of Hereford cattle. My

Overleaf: Being the lone lookout, a sentinel of the herd, "is like being a babysitter," as one cowboy put it. The cattle are upset about leaving their summer home; the territory is unfamiliar to them, and many of them have become separated from their calves. In their nervousness they mill, moo, and bellow until they are settled, and then go placidly to grazing.

family raised Hereford cattle until about 1960. That's all they had. At that time we felt that it was good business practice to crossbreed, and we chose Angus to crossbreed with. We have approximately 50% crossbred cows.

We have a Forest Service lease or permit. We also have some Bureau of Land Management land on a permit, and we lease from the city of Los Angeles. The land is mostly leased by the head by the AUM, or animal unit month, they call it. There's a certain fee. The city of Los Angeles leases by the acre, but all the government ground is on an AUM basis. They go up and figure up how much feed is there and how many cattle it can run, and they determine the AUMs that it will stand. And that's what you're billed for. The cost is approximately the same as keeping the cattle down here for the winter. It's been raised considerably in the last few years. In fact, they had a 10-year plan: the total increase from what we used to pay until the end of this 10 years is something like 400%. Typical government deal. Somebody needed to spend some more money, so that was a good way to raise it. The city land is what we lease for winter pasture, and the summer pasture is leased from the Forest Service. So most of our operation is on leased land. I'd say 80-85% of the ranch is on leased land at this time. All the water we have is free water out of the creeks. The city of Los Angeles does charge us on the lease for a certain amount of irrigation water, but it's very minimal compared to the number of acres.

Years ago it didn't take as many cattle for people to operate. There were just more people and more land. There was a lot of land taken for the national parks: people just had a lot smaller ranches. If a guy had a couple hundred cows, that was a pretty fair deal in those days. He could make a living, but of course nowadays it's a different thing. You have to have five times what you had in those days to do the same thing. Land has been taken out of production and gone into wilderness areas or parks. I think that's true throughout the western states.

Here we have lots of kinds of swamp grasses or sedge grasses. There's a lot of native bunch grass, wheat grasses, and blue bunch wheat grass; they're mountain-type wheat grasses. There's some blue grass, and there are several varieties of clover, mountain clovers. Cattle will eat that wire grass in certain years, when it's first coming up fresh. Of course, it certainly isn't the choice of the cattle, that's for sure. It's not real browsing country. They very seldom eat any of the brush up there. The deer graze on some of it. There is a little lupine. Some little low lupine. It's a kind of a brush that the cattle do eat in the fall. Basically, there just isn't a browsing area like the Cosos, where you have a variety of different brush out there that is palatable to cattle. They could eat it and they liked it and they did good on it. There's really a lot out there — white sage, squaw tea, four-wing saltbrush, hopsage, bitter brush, and buckwheat, and those are the names of just a few of them. There's certainly more. In fact, there is purple sage out there, if you've ever heard of that — Riders of the Purple Sage.

Right: "I know my great-grandfather was a horse thief. He got hung for it. My great-uncle got shot — he went messing around with the wrong woman and got killed." Danny Torres

Doug Mullen

I really like the high country.
I'd be content to live there the rest of my life.

I WAS NINE YEARS OLD when I moved to Olancha with my folks. They were tired of the city life. They were both raised on farms in South Dakota. I really took to the ranch life. I got interested in all the tractors and horses, the whole shot.

The first thing I think I learned about living on a ranch was how to drive a tractor. My dad taught me that. I ran it through the chicken house one time. My chores were to bring in wood and feed the animals. In the summertime when I wasn't going to school we had to bale hay, take care of the cows, and just everything anybody else did. I learned about horses. You name it, we did it. We used to put up the meadow grass then. Meadow grass is just a grass native to an area. Alfalfa is something that has to be planted. We used to bale all the meadows in the summertime. It's not as good as alfalfa. It doesn't have the protein. But it didn't cost you anything to put it up. It was cheap. Most of the water came out of the spring or the creek. When I was a kid there were very few irriga-

tion wells around here. We used whatever came out of the creeks in the summer.

I went to school at Cal Poly in San Luis Obispo for two years. I majored in animal husbandry, and I really liked that. I wanted to learn a little more about cows and that. We lived in a house about eight, nine miles out of town. We called it Sewer Creek. There were nine of us living out there. I think the rent was nine dollars and something apiece. There were some pretty good times out there. We'd all be in bed, and somebody would forget to turn out the light. Everybody would be hollerin', "Turn out the light!" And someone would shoot it out with a gun. We used to ride our horses in the house, just anything you could think of. I lived out there for about a year. All the guys were Ag students. Most of 'em were from ranches.

I was ready to leave after two years. I was ready to go to work. And really, I was asked to leave. It was my first and last talk with the dean. Then I came back to

Lone Pine. The first job I got when I came back was with Jimmy Johnson. We built a road to a gold mine up in the mountains. That lasted about eight months. By then it was winter, and we had to get out of there because of the snow. I've done a little bit of drilling and blastin', operated a little heavy equipment, and carpentered; I guess that's about it.

I like what I'm doing now best. When I was going to college, we used to work for some of the guys around there. I haven't really worked on that many ranches.

If I have to have a title, I guess you'd call it the cow boss. You've got to learn the country and your cows. It takes a while to really know. You usually talk to the owner. He tells you about what he wants done, and it's up to you to do it.

At our busiest time of the year we've had as many as 15 men here. We run about 1200 head of cows and hope every one of them has a calf. We are responsible for the care of our cows. We watch our feed and make sure we don't have too many cows in one spot and not enough in another. We gotta know our country. I move these cows around quite a bit in the wintertime. Once a week I try to ride through them and doctor the sick ones. I make sure their supplement is right and that they're all right. In our operation we supplement their feed in the wintertime. We put out a protein mix. We've got to make sure they're getting their quota of that.

We doctor for foot rot and a lot of pinkeye. And sometimes we run across a cow having trouble calving and have to help her along. Foot rot makes a cow real lame, and she can't get around at all. Her foot and leg swell up. It's caused by a bacteria or virus that lives in the ground. A cow will get a crack or cut in her foot; this virus or bacteria will get in there, and it just starts rotting her foot away.

What I like about my job the most is the cows. I like to work cows, take care of 'em, I like just anything to do with cows. Sometimes if a cow doesn't want to go, we're not going to force her. We just have to sit there.

A wreck is anything out of the ordinary that happens. On a cattle drive, we'll spill cows, or a horse falls on one of us. Anything that's not planned is a wreck. If those cows were tired and hungry and they just couldn't see any reason why they should climb another hill, we're not going to force them to go up there. All the beating and cussin' just is not going to make them go. So it's better to just sit and wait until they want to go.

The hardest job here, the one thing cowboys don't like to do, is build fence. I think that's probably the universal job that cowboys don't like to do. And a lot of them won't do it. But it's just one of those things that's gotta be done every year. Fences are necessary now. Back in the old days everything was more open. We didn't have the population that there is now with everybody competing for a little space. We gotta have fences now, especially in California. There's places in Nevada that are wide open yet. In California we gotta fence our cattle in and fence the people out. Because of campers and hunters, there is so much competition for a little bit of wide-open space. And I think the cows are losing.

I really like the high country. I'd be content to live in a place like that for the rest of my life. It's about as

"I can remember, when I was just a little fella, lying in bed and listening to the windmill — I loved to listen to it go 'round. Creak, creak it would go. The water was pumped into an old wooden barrel that had green moss on it. The water smelled funky, but it didn't taste bad."   (Name unknown)

free as a man can get nowadays. It's just nothing but beautiful wide-open country — quiet, no cars; I guess that'd be it, freedom. I'm never what you'd call bored up there. There's a lot of work, but aside from that there's just so many things to look at. Nothing ever looks the same way twice; it always changes.

It's awful hard for a man with a family to make a good living on these smaller ranches, because the pay just isn't there. A lot of them go on to better things. And a lot of them just don't have what it takes to begin with. The wife could work outside the home, but a lot of guys don't like it. Then too, there isn't that much work available here. Most places furnish meat and free housing. Some places charge you a little rent. But the equipment is expensive. It's like any kind of tool. A saddle will cost $750 now. You'd pay $85 just for a common pair of work boots. Dang pants cost $16 a pair. A man goes through a lot of clothes and that kind of stuff, too. If a guy really likes it, likes what he's doing, then it's worth it. A cowboy hat costs about $50 now. A bill cap doesn't give the protection that a cowboy hat does. A lot of time is spent out in the weather, out in the rain. Get caught out in a rainstorm sometime with one of those bill caps on. A man gets water running down the back of his neck. Cowboy hats are a necessary part of the equipment.

I'm real happy with my life and my wife is, too. It's important to have the kind of family that can live this kind of life. I married a country gal. We've had it all: goats, milk cows, chickens. Both the kids have got their own horses. Our boy is seven and our girl is four. Misty has been riding since she was two years old and Dougie since he was three. Yeah, they do all right.

I don't think I'll ever have a ranch of my own, because it's just too damn expensive. But I do hope to have a few of my own cows someday. Run them here where I'm working or find some grass to lease, something like that. It's something to look forward to, a plan, a goal in life. I'll have a few one of these days.

When I was a kid I used to go with Roy Hunter quite a bit. He has a little outfit here in Olancha and used to run cows out at Hunter Mountain. And he used to catch wild burros and sell 'em in those days. He used to take me with him quite a bit. One time we were out there at what they call the Tin Barn. And we were gathering cows. One morning when we woke up, there was two feet of snow, and we sat there for two weeks. All we had was beans and flour. There wasn't another thing in that camp. We didn't have any salt, nothing to put in the beans. So we ate them beans and, oh hell, we made biscuits and tortillas and did everything to that flour that we could think of to make it taste different.

Roy is a good guy. We used to rope burros, too. The sheepherders bought a lot of them from him for pack animals. And if I'm not mistaken, now this is quite a while back, I think he sold some to Sears and Roebuck. They used to sell the burros through their catalog.

There are people right here in this valley who think a man's pretty dumb if he wants to be a cowboy. But the cattle business isn't the main industry in this valley. In other words, this town of Lone Pine is not solely supported by the cowman. Cattle are the number one export of this valley. Now, there used to be a lot of ore coming out of here. That was the main deal. But most of the mines have closed down. There's just small-scale mining now. I guess you'd have to say that water is the biggest export now, but it doesn't contribute anything to this community, while the cows really do. These cowmen buy a lot of stuff in town. They keep the markets open in the summertime. You'd be surprised at the food bills for the summer when you feed a crew. Cattle are probably the number one export that would bring money back into the valley, although Los Angeles does pay a property tax up here that the county does realize. Cattle bring in about $9,000,000. And a lot of that is spent right here. Some of our big expenses are the fees we pay for the trucks to come in here and ship our cattle, and for our medicine, vaccinations, worming, copper shots, and pregnancy testing. Then you buy supplemental feed in the winter. It's $20,000 or $30,000 a year. Five or six vets are supported in this valley by the cattle industry. There are quite a few people that benefit by it.

Well, probably the main reason a man cowboys is because he likes the life. There's no other reason. It's certainly not a real good paying job. You've got to like it or you couldn't stand it, because the hours are long. It's more than a job; it's a way of life. It's something that you live. You don't have your job and then your social life. It's all the same. You gotta like being outside better than you do being in. And you have to like cows and horses, too. Horses are tools as far as I'm concerned. They're necessary tools, and you take care of 'em the same way you would any of your good tools. That's how you should use 'em. You do get attached to 'em, and you'll like certain horses. But cows are the whole backbone of the operation — not the horses. The cows are what are making you your money. You've got to have that horse to work. It's just like the carpenter needing certain tools to make a living. I think I like the cows better than I do the horses.

There are certain things about a cow that tell you right away that she's not right. You look at her general appearance. If her hair doesn't look good, then you know she's unhealthy for some reason. There's a lot of things that can make her look that way. Of course, there are obvious things. With pneumonia, the cows are usually humped up, and they are breathing hard, maybe trying to breathe through their mouths. We just fill them full of antibiotics for that. And pinkeye is always a problem. The eyes turn pink and get runny. Anything that irritates a cow keeps her from producing and doing a good job for us. If she's got foot rot, that's obvious. I've run into a little mastitis, that's spoiled bag; the cows are usually producing too much milk, and we have to milk them out and treat them with antibiotics.

There are worms, parasites. And there are ear ticks. If a cow is really infested with ear ticks, she will lose her equilibrium, hold her ears down, maybe walk with her head to the side, shake her head a lot, and get thin. Those ticks worry the hell out of 'em. If she has got a whole earful of ticks, and they are in there crawling around, sucking her blood, it's real hard on her. The ticks can kill her if we don't get rid of them. We mix up mineral oil with lindane and shoot it right in her ear. It's a big problem in this valley and in the mountains.

Left: Little Misty Mullen is a delight of wit and curiosity about the American-dream lifestyle. The daughter of the Double Circle L Ranch foreman, her daily round of chores with her mother includes milking goats, bottle feeding lepy [orphan] calves, and dealing with chickens, honeybees, haystacks, and new kittens. Misty has been riding since she was two; her horse "Pinto," now 25 years old, has taught every kid in the area to ride since the early 1950s.

Right: Young Dan is dressed like the typical cowboy as described by Rob Flournoy. "Cowboys always wear long sleeves. Always. You never see a cowboy with short sleeves in this country. And he'll have a neckerchief on. He'll have a good, serviceable, felt cowboy hat on. There's good reasons for all these things. He can water his horse from that hat when the horse can't get to the water; it keeps the sun off his head and the rain from going down his neck. The neckerchief is used as a muffler, washrag, and handkerchief. Tied across the cowboy's face on dusty trails, it keeps the dust out of his lungs. He can use it as first-aid ribbons — to make a sling or to tie splints to a broken leg the way they did for my boy Pearce when a horse broke his leg. It's all got a purpose."

Also, flies will drive 'em nuts in the summer. We spray them about every six weeks for that. If a cow is wormy, her hair will look bad. It'll be dull and won't lay down good. She'll be thin and weak. There are several ways to get rid of worms: bolus pills that we can shove down the cow's throat, paste that we can shoot into her mouth, and an injection that we put under the skin. We usually worm out cows once a year.

I have seen a few cows with hardware sickness. She will have swallowed a nail or a piece of wire, and it will perforate the stomach or something. And you might diagnose it as something else and treat her for a general infection with teramycin, and it doesn't do her any good. Then if you do diagnose it as hardware sickness, the first thing you do is drop a magnet in her stomach and hope to collect that piece of metal. You leave that magnet inside her, and it will hold that metal in the stomach and keep it from traveling and doing damage. Sometimes you can pump her stomach full of mineral oil and hope that she will pass it. If it is a real good cow, like a purebred, we will get a vet to operate and take it out. But for these commercial cows, we don't do that. We have to be careful not to leave any pieces of wire around, because they will eat it. Not intentionally, but they will pick it up with a mouthful of hay and swallow it.

Yes, a cow has different expressions on her face. When she is contented, she's got one. When she's mad, she's damned sure got one. And if she's hurtin', we can see it. She's got a certain one when she can't find her calf. When she's hot, her tongue comes out. I guess you could call that an expression. And cows get scared, espe-cially when a pack of dogs gets after 'em.

Most cows would rather run in the bigger open meadows than they would up in the meadow stringers where the timber is heavier. They would rather be close to water. What would a cow do for 24 hours? If she's in the mountains where it is cold at night, she'll go into the timber country where it's warmer. She'll lay down and sleep. In the morning when the sun comes up, she'll go out and fill up, drink water, and lay down out in the meadow and rest and chew her cud. Then she'll get up and eat a little more, take care of her calf. A cow's main concern is keeping her stomach full.

Cows have a lot of intercommunication with other cows. I don't know how they talk or get their point across, but they do it. I'll ride into a meadow and see maybe one cow there, and she'll have ten, fifteen head of calves laying around her. The rest of the cows will be off drinking or to the salt log or feeding. And that cow takes care of all those calves. And when the other cows get full, some of them will come back, and the one that has been babysitting will go off and eat. That's pretty common.

If you are supposed to have 500 head of cows and you only have 450, and if you know your country real well, you have a pretty good idea where they are. You just start looking and trackin'. Their tracks are the most important guide. I check to see how old those tracks are. The best indication of how fresh a track is, is how fresh the manure is. A cow may have gone through there three or four days ago; but in a particular kind of ground it might look fresh. But if you look at some manure and it's not fresh, then your tracks aren't fresh either.

I can make a pair of cows go anywhere I want them to go. And usually if I'm easy with them and they don't get wild and start charging around, I can talk a cow into going anywhere. I just take it easy with her — sorta just let her think that's the way she wants to go. Sometimes it takes patience and time. I do a lot of meandering around with her.

A leader is a cow that's up in front. It's generally a real good traveling cow or bunch of cows. They know exactly where they're going, and they want to get there. During a cow's life spent here, she may go to the mountains eight or nine times. She knows when it's about time to go in in the spring and time to come out in the fall. A lot of old cows are smart that way. Some of our leader cows will check the gate every morning in the summer to see if it's open and time to go to the mountains. Well, I think cows, like other animals, are creatures of habit. They have their routine. And the closer you can stick to that routine with them, the better off you are.

Their intelligence? I don't think a cow is overly intelligent. I've seen cows think things out. Say that I'm trailin' some cows. Sometimes I'll see a cow that can't find her calf in this bunch. And she tries to go back. If a cow and a calf get separated, they always go back to the last place they nursed. And a lot of times I can talk her out of going back, because I know her calf is in the bunch. I've stopped a cow and had her think it over and had her turn around and go back into that bunch. And then too, I've had 'em when there was just no reasoning with them at all. I think cows are pretty smart, really. They're not by any means the smartest animal in the world. But they do all right. If a calf tries to nurse a cow that's not his mother, that cow will kick him or butt him away. A cow will only let her own calf nurse, generally.

Supposing there are 800 head of cattle in Summit Meadow. Just before putting them away for the night, how safe would I be to walk down the middle of them? Well, it would depend on the cows and how they've been raised — how they've been handled. Say you were to walk down the middle of that bunch and there was a baby calf out there that belonged to one of those cows and you were to start dragging it around. That cow might take after you. Generally, though, she would just turn and run the other way, unless you were hurting her calf. Most of 'em would protect their calves. But as far as walking down the middle of them, I wouldn't be scared to do that. Any of them will fight you, if you get them mad. Roping them and doctoring will get them riled up. That will do it quicker than anything. Sometimes parting one of them that doesn't want to go out of her bunch will get her mad. I was loading a bunch of cows on a truck the other day, and one of them got me down in the squeeze pen. She was just starting up the chute and didn't want to go. I was on foot, and I prodded her with a hot-shot, and she just came right back around and did me in right there. She knocked me down on the ground and walked all over me and butted me around a little bit.

Floyd Lockhardt

*I went around a barn one time with a team of young mules,
and just as I did, a kid came around on a bicycle,
which was as strange as an astronaut back then.*

ONE TIME WE WENT TO TOWN with a load of corn. I was driving a trail wagon. I had four head of mules abreast and two in the lead, and my dad had four and two in the lead. We had twelve head of horses, four wagons. My dad drank more than was good for him, so we loaded his wagons with groceries, coal, corn, and so on. He tied his six head of horses and two wagons behind me, and we started on 35 miles of snow about a foot deep. I was 12 years old. But that would be a little scary now that I'm 65. But I guess I would've known better when I was 12. I made it in one night with the twelve head of horses and four wagons all loaded. You run a while, you cry a while, you sit a while, then you run some more to keep warm, see. But ah, freezing, freezing. I don't know how cold it was. We didn't have a thermometer. All I know is it was freezing. I had overshoes, long underwear, all the clothes I could get on. And I still couldn't stay warm unless I ran. I was sitting on the wagon box, wagon spring seat up there, and got

damn cold, believe me. Finally I got down in the wagon and covered up with quilts, but that didn't work either. The best way is to tie the lines up to the brake and run alongside.

As long as I fed a horse, he'd do good. A horse will stand lots of cold weather if he's fed lots of grain and lots of hay, which we did. We had some awful fine horses. We had some awful fine mules. They were all the transportation we had in 1910. We hauled wood, coal, and grain. We freighted it if we went to town.

At night when we slept, we always tied our horses around our wagon. We slept under the wagon. And the horse's stomping kept the snakes and rattlesnakes from crawling into our bedroll with us. That's right, ain't no bull to that. We slept inside when there weren't so many of us, but times came when some would have to sleep on the ground. With all those horses stompin' and eatin', chances were better against gettin' bit by a rattler.

At home we used to have hayrides when we were

young. When we kids were little, we went to parties or picnics or Sunday School in the wagon. But then, when we got older and went to dances, we all went horseback. Five or twelve miles to the dance. You'd dance all night long and, come daylight, go home.

We made two trips out of Oklahoma to New Mexico. Two trips in the covered wagon. My dad, his brother, and my granddad. They came out and homesteaded and dug the dugout that they were going to live in. And then they went back and gathered the crops and went to Texas and picked cotton and then came on to the homestead. The next year they went with the team and wagon all the way back to Kansas to work in the wheat harvest. It was the only work then. The wheat harvest or cotton picking. Or cowboying. Cowboying didn't pay enough. You never got ahead cowboying. I think my granddad had three wagons. We had one wagon and my uncles had two wagons. And we had many loose horses, driving with the cattle. I don't remember how many cattle — 100, 150 head, I suppose. There were probably 40 head of loose horses and 30 head that worked. We probably harnessed 30 head of horses every morning. Whatever the cattle could eat on the road was all they got, and that's why we'd drive the cattle so slow. They'd eat as they went along, you know. We figured we could cover about 15 to 20 miles a day because we had the cattle with us. Fifteen miles a day, every day, is a long way with the cattle.

It was a picnic all the way. It was all new country. Every night we would stop and picnic, and everybody cooked and ate together. Yeah, as I remember now, there

was nothing bad about it. One covered wagon caught on fire, and it got burned a little. And my dad had a runaway with his wagon one time. I was on horseback. It didn't bother me, but it scared him. We didn't have any sickness or anybody get hurt or anything. Of course, if one of us *did* get hurt, he was just that far from the doctor. We did whatever we could ourselves, and that was it. There was nobody to help. Our mothers were the doctors, and that was it.

Oh! Yeah! We had a nice trip. And then we left our stock and everything and all the extra horses we could and went back for the second trip. On the second trip my dad trailed the wagon. He brought his furniture, chicken coops, and everything tied on the side of our wagon. It's the only way we had to move it. Poor Okies. Whatever we were going to have, **we** had to take with us — a few chickens and turkeys and a few milk cows. That was it, see? Even fence. Whatever we had that we could possibly take with us, we took. There was no place to buy all the stuff. Well, my dad bought a new wagon there in New Mexico. He gave $45 without the box. And that was a lot of money back in those days, $45. So then he built his own box and had his own spring and double trees. I think his double trees came with the wagon. That was standard equipment.

The first cow I ever saw hauled was in a wagon like this. Big team mules had come into town hauling this steer brought for the butcher. And that's the first time I ever saw an animal hauled. He was just put in the wagon and hauled in. The owner drove right down on the main street of town and showed it off, you know.

Eight team mules. It was fancy. The big team all harnessed and the brass spots and, oh, he was a proud man, believe me! Black mules. Big, tall, black mules. Biggest two mules, 16 hands high. Big Gees. At that time those mules would sell for $500 a pair. That was like a Cadillac selling for $15,000 today. Mules were always high. Good mules. Good spanning mules. "Span"; you never say "team." Say team horses and span of mules. Don't ask me why. That's just the way it is. And those old ears just afloppin' as they walked, just aworkin'. Walking right down through town.

We hauled hogs to town. We put on sideboards so we could haul hogs and wheat, corn, and beans; on the return trip we'd haul coal, coal oil, groceries, and whatever. We'd feed cottonseed cake to the cattle. That was the only feed we ever fed a cow in the wintertime. We had no hay to feed them. We'd freight cake, as we called it, made out of cottonseed meal pressed into pellets. It came in 100-pound sacks. We used to freight cake back for the cattle ranchers. The cattle ranchers had so much cake and so much salt and stuff hauled back. They might trade a half of a beef or a whole beef to get several loads of cake hauled out of town for them.

We had a big white corral about the size of a square block. Once, my uncle just let my aunt and two kids off and drove into this corral to unhook a team of broncs. He was always working broncs. And he broke a line just as he drove in, and the horses just started to run. All he could do was just sit and hold them in a circle inside this corral and let 'em run. And he just sat 'till he ran them down. He just sat and held them to the line. Held them in a circle 'til they just run plumb down. There was no other choice.

It was somebody's job every night, if we were freighting out on the road, to grease the wagon. We always had our axle grease and jack, and that's all the tools we'd have right there. The barrel of drinking water for the horses sat on one side, and drinkin' water for the people on the other side.

This is probably a Stewart-made wagon. Ah, Studebaker! Studebaker is the name, not Stewart! Yes! Yes! Yes! Studebaker made the wagon before they made the automobile. Do you know what this is? This chain? It's called a stay chain; with this, if you get one horse stronger than the other, he won't pull the other one back. I can adjust this so that when the stronger horse pulls, he pulls on the front of the axle rather than pull this. There ain't no way for him to pull the other horse back into the wheel, because he'd be pulling the wagon, pulling the wagon ahead.

I went around a barn one time with a team of young mules, and just as I did, a kid came around on a bicycle, which we didn't see often then. A bicycle was as strange as an astronaut. When the mules saw this bicycle, they broke and ran. They ran about a half mile across the pasture. All I could do was hold them straight and let them run. It was scary! The wagon bouncing! It was scary! I mean it isn't something I started. That's for damn sure. But when they do it, I just let them run. That's all a man can do. Ha! Ha! Ha! There wasn't any John Wayne in those days!

Rob Flournoy

*I talk from my heart. My eyes reflect the use
and the care we try to give this range.*

I DON'T BELIEVE I ever in my life went to a beach. Every vacation we've ever had, we've gone to a hotel, been in business meetings, and then got in an airplane or train and got home as quick as we could. It's a good life, so maybe we don't need the vacations because we have them every day. We do enjoy the ranch life. Everything is wholesome. We like to eat good beef. We like to get our milk from the cow. We like to garden. We eat lots of fresh vegetables that are grown close and handy. My dad was never a gardener. He said, "I'd rather raise another calf and pay the gardener for the vegetables." He was always this way, so he didn't raise many gardeners among us. But one or two of us have a wife that'll

Left: "Years ago we had good-sized rodeos here in Likely, right here on our place. My dad and his brothers built the arena and the grandstands. The cowboys would come from all over to rope and ride. But today we can't afford the insurance, so it's strictly a local affair now with a jackpot for the best roper."

Pearce Flournoy

spade a little bit and raise a radish or two, and that's about it.

I think the Flournoys are friendly people, back as far as you want to go. Mother always insisted on family reunions, and she would explain to us that we never had an enemy in the world. We don't have any neighbors that are enemies to us, or we to them either. Our families and neighbors are real close. They've always been close. The ranch that we're on was the Williams Ranch of three generations until the day that the last two girls left. One married a druggist, and one married a man in business in Altures. They sold the ranch to us. We've bought several ranches and let the people live there the rest of their lives. We never took the home until later, if they wanted to live there.

It's tough for someone who's been working for us for 20 years. We do have withholding and things like rockin' chair money that we try to put away for them. We have a former manager that's been with us since

Above: Traditionally, branding is a festive occasion when the ranch owner invites all his cowboy friends to a party held after the work. The cowboys all take turns at cuttin', inoculating, branding, and earmarking the cattle. But the favorite is heelin' and headin' [roping the head and heels in a team effort to drag the calf to the branding fire]. It is all done in the western spirit of a community effort, and you can often hear cowboys brag about how many brandings they were invited to during a season.

Right: In the early years, brands were usually the initials of the owner, but a rustler could easily change a C *to an* O, *an* F *to an* E, *or, for example,* JY *into* OX. *Ranchers soon began designing brands that were difficult to change.*

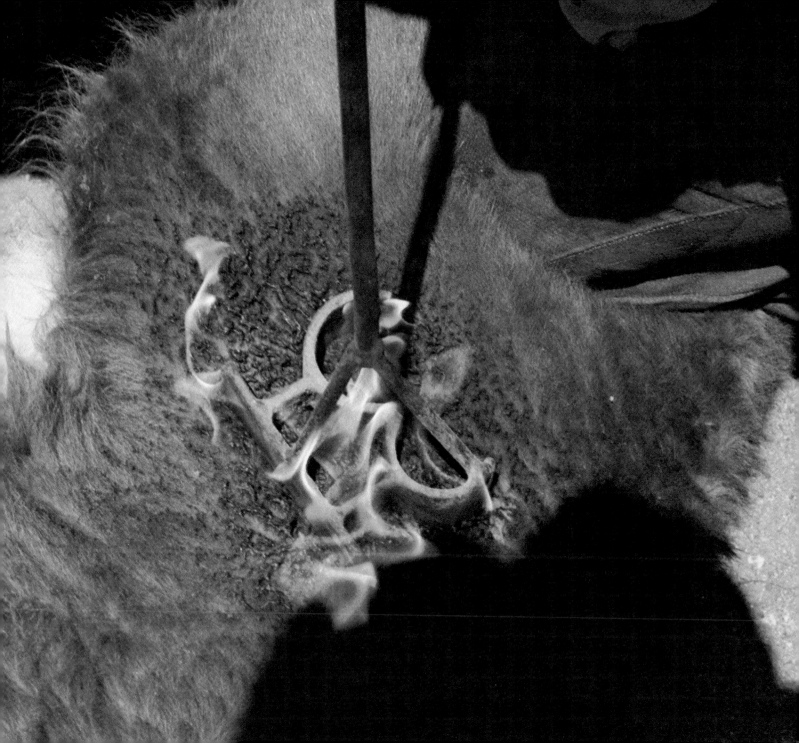

'38. He retired. We had a home over in Likely and just gave him the home and the property to live in. We see that what little money they have is spent on themselves and not for living conditions. It's been real tough to keep people. It has been tough for the last 15, 20 years to keep a man on the ranch, because ranching life hasn't been all that great. Salaries haven't been all that great. If we have a good man, the county can come along and give him more of a salary than we can. They can give him more of a pension plan, more of other things that entice him off the ranch. The Forest Service has done this. We've got a lot of good local men in the Forest Service that were once good ranch cowboys. They know the country. Thank God the Forest Service has a few of them, or the Forest Service wouldn't know a thing about this country. They are a big help. Those fellows know how to talk to the people in the area. Consequently we have better relations with the forestry people.

We have a man here named Bud. He's come back to work, but he's been off. He had worked for us before. He'll stay eight or ten years in different places. And now he's back here; we hope he'll stay here as long as he lives. Years ago, the men would live right out on the ranch and retire on the ranch and die on the ranch. We've got a cemetery over here, full. I shouldn't say "full"; but there are a lot of burials over there of people who have lived on the ranch and maybe chored during their later years because they couldn't go anyplace. A man would have his room, his bunkhouse, a place to stay, and his keepsakes and pictures; his family could come to see him. That's as good a home as you'd want. He'd just stay here until we'd have to put him in a home or he passed away. Then we would have the burial for him and pay the expenses of his funeral — treat him as best we could.

It's hard to talk about the size of the operation. This ranch that I'm on is probably about 9000 acres. Now, in an operation of this size, that would be deeded land. Then I lease 42,000 acres from Weyerhauser Company up near the Oregon line. It's fenced. I fenced it with the help of the government on one side and Weyerhauser on the other. I've had to negotiate permits and leases through them. They've been rehabilitating that range and planting it with trees. I serve on the livestock board with the Weyerhauser Company. They are very interested in grazing, because it keeps down the fire hazard and the competition for their new trees. The grass outgrows the trees for a while, 'cause the trees are little. They're six, eight inches high at first. It takes them three years to get to be two and a half feet high. When they're that high, then they're pretty safe.

We've run experiments up there. The cattle are used to the timber and don't bother trees at all, very little. Deer bother them very little. Porcupines bother them more. And, of course, in some areas you've got horses, which are probably the worst of them all. Horses are out there winter and summer, and they create more problems in a forested area than any other animal. They step on the trees for one thing. The way they step, the way they handle and shift and duck and dodge, they tear up the ground a lot more than probably any animal out there. They also waddle up to the water holes.

We've got about 60,000 acres that we're using — that's both Forest Service and Bureau of Land Management. We're using that in common with other permittees. Neighbors will join you in the use of the land. I'm all alone with Weyerhauser, but the Forest Service and B.L.M. are ranges that we run in common. We turn out on the same days, we ride the same days, and we share in the salting and the range management. The expenses are shared among everybody: any permanent costs that go into the feeds or the reservoirs or water preparations are shared. It takes a vast amount of land to accommodate a ranch. I would say today that if you don't have a $1,500,000 operation, you don't have a self-supplying ranch. I wouldn't think that anybody can ranch like we are in this country with a short growing season. I would venture to say that if his outfit wasn't worth $1,500,000, he could not stay on that ranch and provide for his family and pay his taxes, school bonds, and everything. It used to be $60,000 would buy a ranch 40 years ago. That same ranch today that you could have bought for $60,000 is worth $1,500,000 today.

Earlier we weren't buying anything to improve the ranches. We were using old equipment. We weren't using modern methods. People think we deliberately cut back our herds, but we didn't do this. The banker says, "I want some money," and then you've got to go to your money. At one time we were running two-year-old steers. He'd say, "I still got to have money." So we had to get rid of the two year olds. Consequently the next year all we had was yearlings. We didn't have the two year olds anymore. Pretty quick he says, "Now I want some more money, let's cut this loan down again." So we had to go to the yearlings. We'll sell our yearlings and become a cow-calf operation.

The people that have cow-calf operations today got there because they were forced there. They didn't get there because they could sell a calf for more money than they could a steer. A steer weighs more and he'll bring more. We all love to run steers and heifers and the two year olds, but we got trotted down and down and down with the costs of operation, the money that the banker needed, and the money to pay bills, taxes, schools, hospitals, fixed overhead, and water rights. Insurance is a big problem. Labor is the biggest one. We keep eating into the herd. We're down to a cow-calf outfit. What do we do next?

In the meantime here's our meat market and our short orders and our fast food order commodities and McDonald's teaching the people that a hamburger is a good piece of meat. It's a wholesome piece of meat. You can eat every bit of it. There's no bone in it. It's a beautiful thing. The thing that we've been trying to tell

Overleaf: Dust, sweat, and the sound of saddle leather creaking as the cowboy swings to and fro — it's the same tune in a different century. Nothing much has changed since the trail drives of the 1840s that came out of Texas on the Chisholm Trail to ford the Red River, cross the Great Plains, and drive the longhorn cattle to Kansas and later to California. It was a tough, hard way to earn a hundred dollars for a six-month drive. One cowboy song about the Chisholm Trail went:

I'll sell my horse and I'll sell my saddle;
You can go to hell with your longhorn cattle

people for 30 years is just now getting to them. The consumer has begun to realize, by God, that a pound of hamburger or a pound of meat from a cow or a calf or a bull has the same nutritive value. I don't give a damn if he's raised off of grain, corn, or grass, the meat has the same nutritive values. We've put corn-fed and grain-fed alongside each other, different amounts, fed different rations, and the best people in the taste departments can't tell the difference. But there might be a little bit of texture change.

You've got to put the fat on the outside before you put the marbling in. It's a shame that that's the way it is. People ask, "Why do you overfeed 'em?" Well, it's because you've got to keep that fat on the outside before the marbling goes in. Then you've got to turn around and trim a lot of it off. It's a big cost to trim that fat off.

How did this come about in the first place? When did we get on this grain kick? Well, after World War I and II we had the surplus of our farmers and ranchers. We didn't know how long the war was going to last, and we grew grain and we grew the products that our army needed and our nation needed and our foreign nations needed and our allies needed. We were the only producing country that wasn't being torn up and being raised hell with, so we produced. All of a sudden the war comes to an end, and the farmers have these crops in. We can't shut this off like water. We have a surplus of grain. The government says, "Well, why don't we feed it to cattle? Cattle will do well on it or they'll do great. We'll have a good product." "All right, we'll do that. Now how do we get them to use the product?" "We'll

grade mean." So here comes the grading program. And the only way that any meat will grade high is if the cow's been eating grain.

So that started the feedlots. Feedlots grew and grew and worked well. Feedlots served another purpose. The rancher gets a nice even feed. He stocks his feedlot as he sells off the cattle. He has a market that's ready to go anytime the packer wants it. The packer also has a packing house that can store meat 30–60 days, maybe longer in some cases. Nevertheless, he can supply the market gradually so there are no ups and downs to the demand. The demand is met evenly right along because of feedlots.

The people are talking about hamburger being high and meat being high. Hamburger is beginning to become a premium item. The demand today is for over 50% of our meat today to be hamburger. That's the way people want it now. They like it. They can blend it. They can mix it. It's gotten expensive, so they put extenders into it, and they do everything they can to use this meat in meatloafs and tamales and hamburgers and whatever they want. You can eat it cold, you can eat it raw, you can eat it any way you want it. It's easy to store. It's easy to refrigerate. You can do anything with it, and it's wholesome.

But anyway, the hamburger trade is really the cow trade. Bulls have good red meat, and cow beef is a little lighter in color; they are blended together to give you the good red-looking meat that's called hamburger. They've even graded hamburger now as to certain moisture content and a certain fat content. It's a beautiful packaged meat that no one should be ashamed of. Going to Japan and China, this is what they want. Japan will pay more money for it. They pay a tremendous amount of money for meat there. They pay as high as $35 a pound for meat in Japan. They'll go $12 for a hamburger! You can't believe the amount of money they pay. And the way they grow beef, they only have four or five cows, and some of them will be right in the house. They massage them and comb them and raise them like you would your dog, really. It's beautiful, the Kobe beef is.

It's hard to say who's receiving the lion's share of the dollar. Buyers are demanding more. They want the product weighed. The rancher has to have a cow three years before she produces. He has her for three years before her first calf is born, and every year not better than 80 or 90% of the cattle calve, so you're always carrying 10–20%. He's got bulls to buy, which are expensive. He's got all these things plus other costs. There are death losses all the way along the line. The rates of interest are high. Nobody is getting loans right now on cattle with interest less than 11 or 12%. We've got trucking and handling costs. We've got labor. Labor has to be the biggest cost in the meat business. Safeway turns over its meat every six weeks or so. They run on a very, very slim margin and get the price down so it can be used as a leader, a sale item to get people into their stores to buy other products. They make their profit on something else. They don't make it on meat. *Nobody's* really making money. The public has never believed that the rancher or the farmer is entitled to a profit.

I still dress like a cowboy. Cowboys always wore long sleeves. Always. Never see a cowboy with short sleeves in this country. And he'll have a neckerchief on. He'll have a good, serviceable felt cowboy hat on. There's reasons for all these things. He could water his horse with that hat. He could swat a horse fly. He can make his own shade.

The neckerchief had lots of uses too. The cowboy could put it across his face for a muffler on dusty trails. In the cold weather he tied it over his ears to keep warm. It served as a splint tie in cases where someone had a broken arm or something. He could tie it in strips for medication or for first aid ribbons.

Cowboy boots are designed to pull on easy. When a horse is traveling along, a lot of times he'll kick gravel and sand up high; wearing shoes or oxfords the cowboy would get gravel and sand in his shoes. Even an 11-inch top boot will sometimes get rocks kicked up under the pant leg and over the top, so we get boots 14 to 16 inches. It's a good boot. The idea of a slip-on boot was that if the cowboy got hung up on spurs or saddle or a horse threw him, the boot would come off and he wouldn't drag. It was warmer in the winter and comfortable as we could get. As far as walking, you don't want to walk in them. That's one reason why we said it was no disgrace to grab that saddle horn. Hang on to that damn thing if you don't want to walk, so that you can stay with your horse. It's like the man says, "It'll either be a dehorned saddle or a one-armed man before I get off of here."

Saddles, in our day, were all center fire saddles. By

Left: "I like to brag about my horses. They're just local cow ponies, but we train them to do the job. Trainin' horses is up my alley. I like to ride good horses — it makes ridin' a lot more pleasurable. I'll start a horse in a snaffle bit and go to a hackamore and eventually to a spade bit after years of trainin'. I always give a horse a lot of cues with my hands, feet, legs, and body position about what I want him to do. I don't want him guessin' about what I want."

Tom Fogarty

Right: Young cowboy Cody Christensen takes care of a newborn calf whose cord is still attached. Occasionally, a first-time mother will not nurse her calf, and they must be corralled together until they are "paired up." Cody's dad, "Doc" Christensen, has put most of the local cows back together at one time or another. Doc said, "I was born across the dry lake in Keller, a mining town, during the Depression. It was tough, but we had a strong sense of family and community. I came back to raise my family here after working my way through medical school for the same reasons, and for the Sierra Nevada. There's a good quality of life here."

that I mean they had one cinch. Today we've gone into California styles and more of the Arizona, New Mexico, and Wyoming saddle types. In California we've gone to the double rig, which has a cinch in front and a cinch in back. I can go over in Nevada, and I can tell a Nevada cowboy just because he still rides a center fire saddle, and he still wears the roughout boots with the underslung boot heel, and he still wears a bandana. There will never be any rubber on his saddle horn like they have in California, where these boys are working and competing in rodeos and want a fast stop. In Nevada, cowboys will still be carrying rawhide ropes from 40–60 feet long.

They're still gathering out in the open brush country in common with other users, and they'll bring those cattle to a fire to brand. They take their best cowboy that knows the irons, and they let him go into that bunch with a long rope. He'll catch a calf, and when he brings that calf to the iron, to the fire, he tells those boys on the ground crew who that calf belongs to. He's got six or seven irons in the fire, all different kinds. In the fall when you are gathering cattle you'll find out what kind of a boss you had out there, by the mistakes that are made when calves that have your iron belong to somebody else's cow. In those days it very rarely happened. It happens some today because the boys are a little faster. They're a little more careless, but they're good enough to exchange what they've done when the cattle are mixed. They'll exchange their calves and get their irons and clean up the cattle that have been branded wrong, and so there's no problem. It's not a stealing problem at all. It's not anything but just a mistake.

About the image of the cowboy: most of them will keep their hair cut clean. I like a neat, clean haircut. They'll grow lots of beards out there when it's cold, but when they get to town they like to clean up. Saturday night is the night that they come to town. Most of the time, one guy out of fifteen will own a car. They'll jump on it from all sides and ride into town and then they go to the bars and parties. The big end of them are all single men. They've been disappointed in life or they grew up just naturally being cowboys. Women are just Saturday night fixtures, and they're glad to get back to the ranch, their horses, and possibly a dog. Dogs in Nevada never become too popular around the cattle. They always had dogs around the sheep. But most of the cowboys now are getting more dogs to work their cattle with, to gather with, to drive with.

We haven't got the cowboys we used to have. We used to have some real fine cowboys in the early days. He could go out and cook for himself and make all kinds of biscuits and gravy and good dinners. He could stay for weeks, months, in a cabin, and he was right at home. He had his horses, and the job to do. We don't have that type of cowboy today. The cowboy today has changed considerably. He's got to be where he can see TV at night. He'll have a fine car and he'll have a radio and hot-and-cold running shower and all these things. It's funny. On this ranch, until I was almost 48 or 50, we never had a truck that hauled a horse or a horse trailer. We rode everywhere. If we went up in our ranges, 60–70 miles from here, we got five or six extra horses together with pack outfits. We put our beds and our grub and everything in there and led those horses out. We didn't have stock trucks. We didn't have buses. We didn't have anything running through the country. A railroad train came through about twice a day, and other than that, we just had cattle. It was nothing to have big stampedes out of those cattle when we came down the road. Something like a train would stampede them. So we'd stay back, way back in the hills until that train came through. Then we'd try to get them on across the tracks. We had an awful time crossing the tracks. When the pavement came in, we had to cross highways with cattle. It was a big chore. Our cattle and our cows were now dragging the little baby calves across the highway. They grow up with it now, and we don't have that problem. But in the early days the transformation from gravel to pavement and the coming of more railroads and more buses and more car travel were a real problem to us. People who didn't know livestock came up. Resort people or tourists didn't know how to drive through cattle. They'd drive up and stop and want to get out and take a picture. There's nothing worse. It'll scare the cattle all over, it's a problem. We try to be polite to these people. But you had to break the news to the people that drove up here — that these cattle weren't gentle.

I think the cowboy has a very particular sense of humor. He's seen so much in everyday life, with the livestock, with the horses that he's around. If he doesn't have a good sense of humor, you've got to work him alone. You've got to put him out by himself. He's more like a prospector or a miner or someone who wants to be alone. He's been really disappointed in life or he has an impediment. Maybe he has an affliction or something that he's been teased about or something's bothering him. You've got to see this and overcome it and help him in some way to have a place that he enjoys. These kind of people were a lot of our help. We could see this in people and put them where they would do best. That's what they wanted. They didn't want the city. They were stuttering or they had the shakes or they were nervous, but out on the ranch where they eat three good meals a day and things were wholesome, they went to bed when they wanted to, they got up when they wanted to, and did the things they wanted to do.

When we kids were little, if one of us was sent out to get a cow or a calf, and if he came back and didn't tell the honest-to-God truth or if he didn't do what he was told to do, man, they'd walk right up and get him by the arm off that old saddle and jerk him off onto the ground and give him a Dutch rub right up the back of his neck. They'd just rub his hair, just make him cry. They'd set him back on that saddle and say, "The next time I send you out there I want you to do what you're told to do, and if you're not man enough to live with us, go home. Don't stay out here." Well, it was our pride that kept us there. We knew we'd get it again when we went home, to the tune of the hickory stick.

My son is a good boy. Some kids are just naturally going to grow up and be cattlemen, because they're not going to let you leave them home. Now my boy went to Cal Poly and studied a little legal administration. He took farm practices, horseshoeing, meat cutting, and he learned to fly. Cal Poly is a great practical school. While I was president of the California Cattlemen's Association, I constantly kept after the universities to put in some pre-medicine course work to get more graduate veterinarians. We only have one school here and one in Washington, one in Colorado, and one back in Nebraska. Veterinary schools are scarce, and we're not getting enough graduates out of them. Some of them that do graduate are under-financed, and they go into research and laboratory work or small practice. But we don't have enough in large animal practice, which we were striving for. There were a lot of dropouts. A class at Davis, starting with 90, might wind up with 30 at graduation. Only 2% would stay in large animals. The rest of them would go to small animals or dog/cat hospitals. They didn't have the money to start in large animals. With large animals, the money doesn't come in like it does in a hospital, and, boy, you work day and night and at all calls and in tough conditions.

I didn't tell my son he had to be a cowboy. In my work with public lands, as director and the president of all these damn things, I'd go to some of the agencies and do some work with advisers on crops and various things. They'd ask, "Where's your Master's?" or, Where's this?" I don't have any. Mine is practical knowledge. But I saw that a college education is important. I've been president of the state association and a director of the national association and chairman of several committees with the forestry and public lands and taxation and on the Hayden Brand department.

I've been on various committees and boards, functioning and getting around traveling as much as I do; I'm well known and my activities are down on paper. I've learned from the timber people and the mining people and the cattle people and the water resources people as well as the air people. These people all belong hand-in-hand, and they'd better get together. They'd be better together.

A backpacker will think he adds more money to the society hiking along in a primitive area than a man with 200 or 300 head of cattle out there. He's bought a cane and a pack bag; he put some people to work in a factory to build that. He's exercising and he's demonstrating that he can survive and he's writing a book and he'll get it published. These other people — in timber, mining, cattle — they don't write books. They don't write anything about themselves. They don't publish what ought to be published. That's why it took 30 years to get the public to realize the nutritive value of various meats.

I talk from my heart. My eyes and I reflect the use and the care we try to give this range and how bad we feel when they say we're hurting it. We want that range to look the best it can. We want it to provide the best it will.

Right: The cowboys are doctoring a calf with the scours — dysentery. Afterward, the calf will join its mother. Occasionally a cow will abandon her offspring or die, and a surrogate mother is needed. Since cows identify their calves by smell, some cowboys will spray deodorant on the calf and then give the cow a noseful. It sometimes works, and the mother will come to accept the calf by that smell. Other ranchers tie an orphan calf neck-to-neck with a calf who has a mother; the cow will think they are twins and nurse both.

Buck Elton

And so we say, "Goddamnit Governor Brown,
we just couldn't have made it without your help!"

THE COWBOY DOESN'T WANT ANY SUBSIDIES; he's too damn independent. He doesn't want the government screwin' around with what he does, because they would be tellin' him who he could hire and who he couldn't; they prob'ly would have equal-hiring rights for women. The cowboy is too damn independent, and he has been for the last hundred years. He just don't want any interference. He'll just tough it out if it gets bad, and it usually does. I always say my partner is so used to hard times that when things get real good for him, he'll run down a barbed wire fence just to bully himself up, because he's never had it good.

Now we had a drought in California for over two years, and a lot of us got hurt by it. Governor Brown set up a Disaster Relief Act, which was a $10,000,000 fund set up by the Assembly to handle those hurt by the drought. We felt that we lost $150,000 over a two-year period since we didn't have as many calves as we should because the herd wasn't as healthy, due to lack of feed. For example, we put out 500 steers to winter feed: they went out weighing 400 pounds, and they came back six months later weighing 400 pounds. So they didn't gain anything. They should have weighed 600 pounds. And when a steer doesn't grow a normal growth, he never will grow. The buyers know this. It's not a fat little steer, and its bones have probably outgrown its body. It doesn't come out as good for the buyers, so they pay less.

So we felt we lost $150,000 due to a lot of factors directly related to rain, feed, and whatever, and we applied for the relief fund and filled out all the bureaucratic forms. I must have made $150 worth of phone calls to Sacramento and one trip up there to get information. They evaluate your claim and pay by a formula of how much land you own and what your taxes are. It's a real complicated deal. Well, we got all through filling out all those forms in compliance with the regulations and, sure enough, they paid us! I got the check on the wall. It's for $8.82! And so we say, "Goddamnit Governor Brown, we just couldn't have made it without your help!"

All the cowboys in this part of the Owens Valley decided to have a horse race. It was a joke at first, but they each anted up $25 and had a horse race on a Saturday morning down on the 3000-foot-long airstrip. There must have been 50 riders in the thing. They came from all over with their horses. Some fine horses came out here. Butterworth's daughter brought a race horse up here from Santa Anita with all the silks and a little saddle; obviously it was the fastest horse in the world.

They all came out with their horses. We got the pickup trucks on the runway. We had a ol' boy by the name of Jack Mickavac who had a bugle. He was into his cups early in the morning. So then Roy Hunter and Bob Swandt rode up on two horses. One horse was 21 years and the other was 22. Everyone wondered just what in the hell they were doing, paying $25 to enter those old horses. Jack Mickavac stood up in the back of a pickup and blew his bugle. All the guys lined up, and someone shot off a gun and off they went. Well, everyone went into a dead gallop except Bob Swandt and Roy Hunter, who were holding their horses back, and they were having a hard time doing it, too, 'cause their horses wanted to charge down that old runway with the rest of them. But they managed to hold them in check until the rest of the runners went on down to the end of the runway and kept on going (probably to Little Lake): nobody turned their horses around for the leg back to the finish line. This is because once a

bunch of horses start running out across the desert, nothing is going to stop them. Anyway, all them horses went out to the end of the runway and still kept going south. They never could turn them around. Roy Hunter and Bob Swandt trotted down to the end and trotted back. About halfway back they mildly raced each other, and Roy won by about a half a head. I'm sure they split the money, and I'm sure they had it figured all the way. And the woman with the race horse? The last time we saw her she was headed for the next county, tryin' to stop that damn thing! Great day in Olancha!

Overleaf: "Our granddad decided to settle here in the South Fork around 1865 because of the free open country, the amount of water, and the friendliness of the Pitt River and South Fork Indians. He had four boys, including our father. We've all got a piece of the original ranch 125 years later, and we make our living being cowboys just like our granddad. Rob Flournoy

Roy Hunter

Here comes this cow! Just head over heels!
I don't mean rolling sideways —
I mean going just like a ball — end-over-end!

I MADE A LIVING practically all my life mustanging. Whatever we caught, we'd trade and sell. We just stayed at it for eight, ten years. That's all we did. Some people want colts or somebody wants a mare or somebody wants something special. We roped 90% of them, so we could be choosy. If we knew that somebody wanted a young colt to break, well, that's what we'd go try to get. We knew we had a market for it. After we traded horses a while, people came to us and more or less put in orders for what they wanted. When we got the order, we knew what to go and get. Most people wanted young mares or studs. The people didn't care as long as they were young.

The only thing to do with the old ones was to send them to the killers. That's a no-no now. But in those days there was what they called "the killer market," where we'd take a mare that was too old for somebody to break. The only place to take 'em was to the killer market. There wasn't much percentage for me in catching killer horses. I'd catch young studs and young mares and colts — pretty young colts — because that's where the market was. Some people think that weeding out some of those horses helped the herd.

I've got to give you a little history. When I went into the service, my dad had a lot of horses, like 150 head of mares, and he was getting pretty old. They were pretty well-bred horses, good horses, but they were wild. They got wild because he couldn't handle them. He couldn't control them. He couldn't ride, and there was no one available to help him; so when I was gone, they got out of hand. The only way we could treat them was just like wild horses.

There aren't very many wild horses on Hunter Mountain now — very few. They're all gone. They've been shot, killed, and whatnot. The Park Service has eliminated a lot of them. As you get farther north into Nevada and even in Arizona, there are quite a few wild horses roaming around the country. But in each little area the horses are different.

People talk about mustang horses. These are domestic horses that have gone wild. If you start off with a good breed and get new blood in it, you get good horses. If they were scrubs to begin with, then they end up being scrubs. Sometimes to improve the herd we'd let a good stallion out there. Any kind of new blood improves them. It doesn't take very long for them to get inbred. Anytime you put new blood in there, it always improves the breed. They're always stronger and more aggressive than the inbred ones. The Park Service was shooting some of the horses. I've never known the Forest Service to ever shoot a horse, but the Park Service has. It's in their policy to eliminate those horses. One hundred percent eliminate them. They don't want to thin them out. They want to get rid of them. I know it for a fact, but I doubt if it's public record.

The Park Service got an injunction against me for grazing livestock within the Death Valley National Monument, and we were in a lengthy lawsuit over it for about eight years. The windup of it was that they took about half of the range away from me, and I got caught in the middle. We ran horses. Half of the range is what's called B.L.M., Bureau of Land Management. We didn't have a horse permit, but we had a cow permit, so we kept the horses within the Monument, which the B.L.M. didn't have any jurisdiction over. When I lost the lawsuit, they got the injunction against me, and they went in and killed the horses.

You have to know what you're doing to catch a wild horse. You have to be on horseback. You have to have good horses — horses that can run and run in tough ground. And you've got to know the country. Catching a wild horse is something you learn how to do. There are a lot of different ways. The way that I myself did it more than any other way was to just build a loop and go out there and rope the one I wanted. But I had a market for everyone I roped. I knew what I could do with it. That's the reason that I like roping better than foot trapping; I never knew what I was going to get in the foot trap.

A mustang's the greatest general in the world. It's pretty hard to outsmart him. You really have to outdo him. Mustangs have got so many tricks that every time I'd think I knew them all, I'd get hold of one that'd teach me a new one that I'd never seen before. He never gets himself in a position where he can be cornered. He'll never go down a deep canyon. He'll always take the ridge. You can hardly make him run downhill; that is because he figures there's a trap there. He'll always contour and pretty well stay out of any big wash or deep canyon. He sees everything and he hears everything. The only way to get the jump on him is by knowing the country.

And horses follow patterns. If a horse runs in a certain circle and he gets away, the next time I jump him he's going to run in that same circle. I can cut him short because I know he's going to go in a certain direction. I get over there, and I gained a lot of ground on him. I've had a lot get away from me, but it was usually in rough ground or maybe in timbers where I couldn't see him. There's no time for tracks; I just stay with him.

I'd build a loop and be sitting there, the saddle cinched

up and my horse knew it, too. Right away he knows you're gonna go. You run behind the mustangs. You can't run alongside them or they'll turn off. You have to drop in behind them 'til you get in close enough range to rope one. You stay eight, ten feet behind him, usually. It's pretty hard to get within six feet of one. You have to throw the rope ten, twelve feet. You've got to throw it hard. You throw it right at him; you don't let it drop. You've just got to *throw* it on him. I mean you can't let it float.

A lot of people fence off the water and just leave one corral open. I've done that myself, too. When the mustangs came to this certain corral, we would just drop a curtain behind them on a slipknot. We just pulled a trip rope, and the curtain would fall behind them like a piece of canvas. Later, nearly everybody started using what's called an automatic gate. It's a spring-loaded deal. A mustang can squeeze through and open it up, but when he tries to come out, it tightens up on him. That way nobody has to be there. It's a lot better. When we're water trapping wild horses, if we build a fire or smoke a cigarette or do anything, the mustangs smell it. They can smell it a long way off, and they won't come in. They just go ten miles away to get a drink. So the automatic gate works a lot better.

Sometimes I'd make a foot trap and bury it in the ground. The principle is that it's just like a box and the horse steps through it. I'd tie a piece of truck inner tube and stretch it really tight, and I'd have a rope around that box. When the horse steps through it, it triggers the inner tube to snap the rope across the foot. The rope

is tied to a limb or something that the horse can move a little. It isn't so solid; he can drag it off a little way. Then it doesn't hurt him. If it was tied to something solid, he could break a leg.

Those are the main ways we trapped them. It sure was exciting. It's just like fishing or anything else. I enjoyed it. It was a bigger thrill for me to catch a big stud than it was to go hunting deer or kill anything. To be able to sit and rope a mustang and tie it down and get it in the corral was, to me, a lot more thrilling than other kinds of sports.

Very seldom does one ever get away. I've lost a saddle before. Once I went to move some cattle and I'd forgotten my bridle, so I was riding with just a halter; I was just going to move the cattle. I saw a young colt. A man here in Lone Pine wanted to buy just such a horse about two years old, and I saw him. I thought, whoa, if I catch this horse, I'll sell him to that guy. So I roped the young stud. My horse had only this halter on, and I was a little bit concerned. We were running along downhill, and I gave him a pull and I hollered, "Whoa!" Well, it startled him, because I'd never done that to him. And when I did that, he just buried his tail right in the ground! Man, he just stopped like he'd hit a brick wall. He stopped so hard and the other one was running so fast that it just jerked this saddle right off over his head. And it was a brand new saddle. Down through the wash we went and I still had my [rope] turns on. I stayed with the saddle, but my saddle didn't stay with my horse! I had a brand new rope. I didn't want to lose that. I could have let the colt go, but the saddle finally dragged against some brush. I got him stopped and tied down. That was one time.

Oh, we've had a lot of wrecks, but I was only hurt once. I broke a bunch of ribs. Where I got in trouble was when I got a bad horse that fell with me.

Joy and I stayed with mustanging for about eight years after we were married. Of course, I'd mustang'd a lot before. But she and I used to go together all the time. We lived on Hunter Mountain and ran a few cattle. We didn't have anything to keep us in the valley: none of our kids were old enough to go to school. We just lived up there and would go wherever the wild horses were. She's pretty handy. A lot of times when I'd take her with me, we'd have two good horses. I'd go rope something. And instead of taking time to tie it down, I'd take my turns and let Joy get in my saddle. And I'd jump on the other horse. Then I'd run and rope another one without losing time. If we got into a bunch of horses that were running pretty good, she'd rope one with me. Then I'd tie mine down and go over and help her to tie hers down. She roped quite a few.

My grandfather came here in 1868 or '69. He'd been a Confederate officer. At one time the Confederacy was getting its silver bullion from Virginia City, Nevada. So as a young man, he'd made a trip to Virginia City. He was always interested in mining and livestock anyway. After the Civil War when he got home, there was nothing there for him to do. So he just saddled up a horse and came to Virginia City, Nevada, and he met my grandmother. He had a lot of pack mules in and was interested in mining. After that he was always a rancher. He had a ranch in Lone Pine and then one right here. I don't think he ever worked for anybody that I know of.

At Cerro Gordo he ran smelters, but he was also mining his own property at the same time and packing water to the town of Cerro Gordo. That's really how he came to the town. He had 100 or 150 head of mules. And the town didn't have any water. So he packed water, and that's the reason that he went to Hunter Mountain. He had mules that needed rest and time off, so he went to Hunter Mountain. He was raising mules and running other mules over there. It was known as Hunter Ranch, but they call it Hunter Mountain now.

My dad was born in Lone Pine. He had three brothers and one sister, but they all died fairly young. He told me he owned his first bunch of cattle when he was just a little kid. I don't know how he got in the cow business. But he bought a ranch and he homesteaded, plus he had Hunter Mountain. I don't know if he got that from my grandfather or what happened there. He ran cattle in the High Sierra in the early days. They kicked him out of there because of a little argument; he got on the wrong side of a political fence. Then he just concentrated on running cattle on Hunter Mountain and over in Death Valley and in the Koweechee Mountains of Nevada, south of Silver Peak. He sold all of Hunter Mountain and the part of Death Valley where Scotty's Castle is to the Johnson who financed Death Valley Scotty. That had been the center of the cow operation.

My dad and I have worked together ever since I can remember. The first incident I can really remember was a time when we left Independence. We were riding Hunter Mountain, and we had left in the afternoon and got out, way out in the desert. I fell asleep and I fell off the horse. I was laying on the ground. I guess I wanted to cry and everything else. But it felt so good to lie on the ground, I just went to sleep. Later he woke me up. I don't know how long I slept, but he let me stay there and sleep. I probably was five, six years old.

We used to go out there and stay all summer. We'd take a pack outfit and go and stay and take care of the cattle. Usually he'd have somebody else working for him, too. Quite a few of the Indians would work for him. We had several line cabins, but the main one was a log cabin right on top of Hunter Mountain. It was the best place to camp because it was cool. We had a pretty good meadow there for horse feed. There was no road. You had to do everything on horseback. It's high desert country; it's nearly 8000 feet high. There was a lot of pinyon timber, heavy timber, and there's small meadows that were anywhere from two up to forty acres. The only things we ever had out there were mountain sheep and, of course, mountain lions, coyotes, things like that.

My dad never stopped because it got late or he was tired. To him there was no such thing as an 8 or 10 hour day. He only stopped when the job was done. If we were 40 miles from camp and couldn't make it back, we just stayed there all night and started work again the next morning. He was a very fair man, with a lot of patience for both men and animals. He had a lot of patience with kids, too. He would try to teach me all he could, but he never really forced anything on me or made me do

something that I wasn't willing to do. In fact, he made me want to be willing. I don't know if I'm a cowboy, but he did his best to teach me all he could.

I don't mind being called a cowboy. I might put my occupation down as "rancher" and let it go at that, because I don't work for wages for cow outfits. I think if you're going to be a cowboy, you're working for somebody else. But when you're running your own outfit, there's a lot of things besides cowboying. In fact, one of my dad's sayings was, "There aren't no more cowboys. The only way you can get along now is to be a mechanic and a baloney artist along with it." It's not just riding a horse anymore. It used to be that that was everything. We didn't have a truck to haul our saddle horses in. We didn't have to worry about a truck. We went with pack outfits and saddle horses, and we didn't have anything mechanical. But we couldn't do that anymore and survive. It's gotten to the point now where we have to run a truck and we've got equipment and we've got things to take care of. It's just not being a cowboy.

One year Byron Burkhart and I were standing guard on cattle. We got them up to a place called "The Chute." It was just as steep as it could be; it wasn't a cliff, but it's the next thing to it. It got late, and we knew that if the cattle came down we'd never get them back up again, so

Right: Roy Hunter and his son-in-law Dan Anderson share the hard work on the Hunter Ranch, which Roy's granddad started in 1869. He had originally come out West to pick up a silver shipment from Virginia City for the Confederate Army, to help finance the Civil War.

we decided to build a fire. Byron got behind a big tree and built a fire.

I said, "You know, if they roll a rock off up there, dark as it is, we won't see it, and it's going to wipe us out down here!" About midnight, I imagine, I heard a thunk, thunk, thunk. We hollered back and forth to each other, "Here comes a rock! Watch out!" I had a big fire going and he had a big fire, and right between us, here comes this cow! Just head over heels! I don't mean rolling sideways. I mean going just like a ball, end-over-end. And she came by us just like you'd turn a tire loose going down there. Well, we stayed behind the tree all night. At daylight I walked down about a quarter of a mile and I found her. All to pieces. She'd rolled off about a half mile and I don't mean rolled sideways. I mean end-over-end. That's how steep it was!

The first or second time we ever came down, there had been a big washout. The willows had been smashed down with the snow. The cattle got going down there trying to walk over those willows. We had 60, 70 head. They just walked out on those willows and the trunks just all caved in. It took us about a half a day to get the cattle on their feet and get them out of there. That was probably the worst thing that ever happened. This country is all right if you understand it, but it can get pretty cruel to you, too. This is pretty tough country for raising cattle. I never had money enough to leave.

Our brand is Bar 26. It came from Shenandoah Valley. My grandfather came out here to Virginia City. He was an officer, so he had the horse that was his own private mount, and he rode that horse from Virginia to Virginia City, Nevada. The horse had a 26 brand on it, so that was it. My dad started branding with it, and he went ahead and recorded it with the state. When I bought him out, I bought the brand. A straight bar across the top with a 26. Originally it didn't have a bar on it. Just the 26. But when I bought him out, he'd let it lapse for a year sometime back in 1895 or 1900, so they wouldn't register it. They wouldn't re-register it in my name unless I put a bar over the top of it. That brand's over 100 years old now.

Right: A pickup man at Cotton's Flying A Rodeo hazes a steer into the corral. The lariat is not just any piece of rope. It is made of carefully braided nylon and must be stiff enough so that when a cowboy pays out a broad loop and then sends it flying toward its target, the loop stays flat and open. The original Spanish lariat was made of braid-rawhide and was 60 feet long, but it was expensive and delicate. Most early American cowboys turned to grass that was twisted rather than braided, and used it until nylon was invented.

Callie Thornburgh

*I don't get on horses until I know they are really relaxed
with me and are not going to be frightened.*

WHEN I FIRST GET A HORSE, I like to get his confidence
and get him to like me. I don't ever want him to be
afraid of me. I want him to trust me and to respond
to me. So my first steps are a lot of touching and handling, brushing, just messing around with the horse,
picking up his feet, getting a rag, brushing it over him
so he's used to things — things a person does putting a
coat on him and putting the saddle pads on him and
the saddle.

When I first put a rope on him, I'll put a halter on
him and I won't tie him up for the first couple of days.
I'll just hang on to the rope and pet him and kind of
lead him around a little bit and make him come to me
and feed him, and then I'll tie him up. I have a good
halter and a good rope. If he fights it, he learns that
he can't get away so he never tries again, usually. When
I tie him up, I step back and get a good 10 to 15 feet
away from him so that when he is fighting the rope, he
relates it to the fence and the rope, not to me. Then when
he is calm and settles down, I walk up to him and pet him
and say, "Okay, it's all right." I try not to ever make
him associate me with any pain that he has, and I use
a lot of lunging because when you lunge, you can teach
voice commands and teach him to respond to you without your being on his back yet. I can teach him to walk,
trot, canter, roll, and turn around before I get on him,
so I'm just that much farther ahead. When I get on him,
he knows the voice commands. When I stop a horse,
I say "whoa" and try to use the same tones all the time,
and he gets used to that.

The last month of training my horses, I train the
rider along with the horse to teach him my aids and my
commands, too, so he can take over and get along with
the horse right away.

*Right: The water supplied by the old watering hole at the Cabin
Bar Ranch is essentially free. Joining the growing list of modern
economic problems, however, is the high cost of electricity to
pump it out of the ground — about $1,000 a month.*

The time that it takes to get to the point of riding depends on the temperament of the horse. But usually it takes from a month to six weeks. I don't like to rush them. I don't get on them until I know they are really relaxed with me and they are not going to be frightened.

Today I was making a horse respond to the bit. When I was lunging him, I had both reins tight on each side to check his head so it was vertical to the ground to teach him to give to the bit, not to pull against it. When you pull on the bit, you want him to bring his head with it. You don't want him to pull back on you. I have the lunge line connected to the head stall on his nose, not to the bit. Right now I check him up on each side to teach him to bend his neck and follow the rein. If I pull on one side I want him to follow that rein around and turn.

Today my dad's going to hold him the first time I get on him, because I don't ever want him to know what bucking is. I never want him to get a chance to get me off. I'm going to ease into the stirrup and talk to him and pet him. I'll put one foot in the stirrup and kind of move around a little bit, pat my hand on the saddle, and pull on the reins, just get his attention, to make him look at me so he knows I'm going to climb aboard. I'll put all my weight on one side, but I won't throw my leg over yet. I'll kind of just sit there for a minute, then I'll go down, and then when I go on I'll throw my leg over, sit down real easy, and just kind of talk to him for a minute and move around. I move around a lot in the saddle, move it back and forth before I make him take his first step.

This is a lot different from the old way of just tying him to a fence post when he's a mustang and letting him buck all day and then climbing on him with three cowboys twitching him and biting his ear. It's a lot different. You want to get the horse's confidence. You don't want to scare him. In those days they broke a horse. They rode it until it was too tired or just too confused to do anything else.

Now when I get on him, he's going to know what I want him to do. It's not going to be any surprise at all. In the old days the horses did what the cowboy wanted him to do because they were afraid of him. Now my horse does what I want him to do because he wants to please me.

Right: "You can't send a guy to do anything unless you know what you're talking about. It's best if you take him and show him how you want it done. And you can't make a guy work any harder than you're going to work — it's just that simple. But you have to keep them happy; you can't just push a guy around."
Pearce Flournoy

Left: Hunting for the horses is a task that falls to one cowboy each morning. In Brown Meadow below Olancha Peak, there are many hiding places for the horses who would rather eat grass all day than work for their grain.

Right: Wind-drawn water is pumped from wells dug by hand. Windmills, their tall forms punctuating American cattle ranches, are seen less frequently in this generation. But Jug Perez, cow boss of the Onyx Ranch, a real western outfit, tries to keep his in repair. One old buckaroo told of climbing to the top as a kid and turning the blades by hand when there wasn't any wind. "I've seen cowboys thrown off when a wind came up, but I'd just hang on and ride around and around 'til the wind died. It was fun."

STORE

TOP ... AT THE TOP
OF T ... IN KERNVILLE
SE ... HE KERN RIVER
V ... OVER 48 YEARS

Billy

I reached up there and didn't get a hold of nothin'!
Come back and damn if I didn't blow a pedal.

I WORKED IN THE PICTURE BUSINESS for a good many years, but I can't say that I liked it too much. There are a lot of phonies in the business. I was wrangling. Every time you'd see a horse, a wrangler is there. You meet some good people, and there are some bad ones. I can't really remember too many good times in the picture business. The people are a whole different breed. They

Left: A bucking Brahma bull ride lasts only eight seconds, if you can stay on that long. The 1,500 pound, fast, powerful, and dangerous animal is responsible for more serious injury than animals in any other event. He often attempts to gore the rider after bucking him off. The loose-hided, spinning, kicking, bucking, furious bulls are too fierce for horse-mounted pickup men. Instead, clowns are used as "bullbaiters" to distract the bull's attention while the cowboy heads for the fence. The dangerous occupation of bullbaiting involves dashing between cowboys and charging bulls, stepping inside with a spinning Brahma to get a rider off, and playacting to make the deadly game seem amusing to the crowd, some of whom believe that the clown is there just for laughs.

think they're really good hands, but they're not. I'm not saying they're all that way, but a lot of them are. There are some good hands in the business, like H. P. Evitts. He is a world-champion roper.

I made $16,000 in 60 days once. My wife figured it up for me. But you don't work too often. It's real spotty. Once they get to know you, you can work pretty steady. But nobody knew me. I could have made more than that if I was a stunt man. I never did any stunts. I did a little blind driving. A lot of times the actors don't know how to run a team, so you have to have a blind driver that does it. You have to cut a hole out of the front of the wagon and put in some cables for lines. You drive instead of the actor. The actor just sits up there and holds the lines. It looks like he's drivin', but he's not.

I love to ride buckin' horses, and I love to drink. And anybody will tell you that you can't ride buckin' horses and drink. Anybody that rodeos a lot will tell you this. It's a tough game. You got to ride your ass off, and you

Left: Billy

got to cover a lot of country. I rodeo'd for a little while. I liked it, and I would like to go back to it. I got my permit card in the RCA Rodeo Association a couple of years ago. I love to ride buckin' horses. I won some money at it, too. I won my circuit, you know. They have it divided up in circuits.

This is the belt buckle I won for the first prize. This is from the Turquoise Circuit. It takes in Arizona and New Mexico. They've got some pretty good bronc riders come out of there. I went to three rodeos in Arizona and New Mexico, and I won two of them and came in second in one of them.

I was ridin' a big old mare and I bucked off her. A guy told me I had my saddle too far forward. I reached up and I didn't get a hold of anything. If you're familiar with ridin' broncs, you come up with your spurs and put them into the horse's shoulder when he is coming down to the ground. You've got to get a hold of something, otherwise he blows you right back. You've got to have your spurs in him. I mean, just as hard as you can. That way, when he hits the ground and breaks for another jump, it doesn't throw your feet back too far. And that's what happened to me! I reached up there and didn't get a hold of nothin'! Come back and damn if I didn't blow a pedal [lose a stirrup]. From then on it was just me kind of fightin' my ass to stay in the middle of that old horse. But anyway, at the other two rodeos I was in I won both of them. I won pretty close to $800 in Santa Fe and over $300 in New Mexico. That's when

I filed my permit. Ever since then I've been RCA, and I won the circuit the same year. I went to Little Wilcox Rodeo (a little pumpkin roller's rodeo). I drew a good bronc and rode him good. I was really proud of myself. In fact, I'll tell you how proud I was of myself. You know, I told you when I rodeo I don't drink; well, that night I got drunk.

We kept track for a while of how many broncs I was ridin' when I was learnin'. We put on a little rodeo of our own, and we figured I was on pretty close to 600 head right there. And since I have been rodeoin', I can't tell how many I've been on. I remember one stretch, when in twelve days I got on twelve head. One day I got on two, and this was when I was winnin', too. If I wasn't winnin', I was placin'. If you can place, you can keep travelin'. If you're winnin', you can travel harder. That's the way it is. And this was on my honeymoon! When I won that $800, I went home and got married.

I didn't even know I was going to get married. She went with me to a bunch of rodeos. We'd go to those little towns, to those little motels; people were always lookin' for the ring on her finger. Once in awhile they would ask, "How come she don't have a ring?" "Oh, she, uh, left it," I'd say (laughs). So I figured I'd buy her a ring. It was a hell of a ring, you know. And $250 for a poor cowboy is a hell of a ring. She doesn't even wear it now. But I kind of love her.

I quit that picture business for cowboyin'. In fact, this year I could be makin' lots of money, because the outfit I left is covered with jobs. I could be workin' every day. A year like this year I could prob'ly make $30,000. But I don't want it. If I had a bunch of kids, I would do it in a minute. But I want to ride buckin' horses again. I'm only 23 years old and I want to ride buckin' horses and I want to learn how to cowboy.

I want to learn it all so that when I go back to that kind of business no one can say, "Well, son, you don't know nothin'!" When I go back I want to know that no one can beat me in the business. I don't want to brag, but there were very few that could outride me in the picture business.

I do know a little about horses. I learned some of it from my dad. We owned a bunch of horses and a couple of milk cows. But I learned most of it from an ol' boy by the name o' Gail Bell. He's from up north in Montana. We came down into this country and ran a dude outfit. He's a hell of a hand around horses. And from what I hear, he's a hell of a hand around cattle.

My wife, Davine (I tried callin' her Davey for a while, but she didn't like that), she worked for us. We started a rodeo. You know where Old Tucson is? We had a string of old saddle horses there (dude horses), and they built a little arena there and we rodeo'd five nights a week for the dudes. It was a little one. Not near as big as a regular rodeo. We didn't rope. We started to rope some steers once, but we stopped after a while 'cause none of us could rope. Like me today, I can't rope worth a damn! But we got to ridin' broncs, and a bunch of the boys came out and rode bulls, and a few came out to ride bareback horses. We got on a lot of broncs. I got on over 500 or 600 in the four years I was there.

After I started ridin' broncs, Davine decided she wanted to ride. This was before we were married. She was drivin' the stagecoach the dudes rode around in. And she wanted to ride broncs. She'd use my bronc saddle; it's a lower profile saddle, without any horn to get in the way. She'd get on them, and they'd buck her ass off! Boy, it was funny! But then I got scared after watchin' her buck off so many times. She did ride a few of them. She does have a little talent. She was a lot heavier then than she is now. She prob'ly weighed 20 pounds more, and I didn't want to see her get hurt. She's got a heart of gold. I'd place her up with anybody to try anything tough. I really would. Today they tried to give me a re-ride on that Brahma bull. That was my buddy's, Jim Cook's, little joke. He wanted to see me ride that mean son-of-a-bitchin' bull again. He told the judge I didn't get a fair ride. Can you imagine? I didn't get bucked off, so he wants to see me ride again to see if I get bucked off the next time! My wife comes up and says, "You ain't going to get on a re-ride. Give him to me!" And she meant it. She might not go the limit, but she'd try! That's one of the reasons I like her so much. Because she's got more try than any person. She doesn't give up!

Right: "Wild cow milking is a real pumpkin rollers [small town rodeo] event, and it's just about the funniest thing ever. A couple of cowboys run after a cow. One holds it by the head, while the other tries to milk it with one hand while holding a small can in the other hand. All the while they dodge the hooves, tail, and other movements of a very discontented cow. Then the cowboy's got to be the first across the finish line with the milk. Ever try runnin' in cowboy boots?" David Riggoli

Overleaf: "One time, when I was a little kid, the ranch foreman Les and I were out after some cattle. We were trying to gather the remnants from the desert, and we knew an area where there were probably a few cattle runnin'. It was right on top of a peak, and the cattle could have gone the right way or the wrong way, it just depended on how we jumped them. We came up over a rise and saw the cattle grazing down the wrong side of the slope. When they first saw us, they kinda jumped. They were alerted. In my position, I had to get down around the bottom side to keep them from going the wrong way. I held the cattle up just right. I just happened to get lucky and stopped them and headed them back the right way. Les pointed out that I did a good job, and it really stuck in my mind to this day because I wasn't used to getting praise."

Richard Rudnick

Cowboy dances and rodeos go together just as naturally today as they have since frontier days and square-dancing. The entire community, people of all ages, attend and enjoy the same dances and music. Cowboys rarely take off their hats anyway, but this dance was so crowded that there would have been no place to put them.

Richard Rudnick

I don't really care if my kids become cowboys.
I just want them to have the opportunity to do what they want
and be happy at what they're doin'.

I WAS BORN WALKING DISTANCE from the ranch I'm running: in Weldon, in the Neal house built by an old Irishman. It's ancient, over 100 years old, and a landmark around here. When I was growing up I worked here on weekends and in summertime and in the feedlots in Bakersfield. I worked with cattle and around cattle all the time.

My dad was in the cattle business, and he made us get out and work. We didn't have any choice. My dad was about the biggest influence in my life. He taught me hard work and a lot of go. He goes 90 miles an hour all the time running cattle on the Fort Ligget, a large ranch over on the coast. He leases the land from the government. He's got a steer and cow-calf operation. He's also got a couple other ranches in San Luis Obispo County that he's running too. His background was in the cattle business, meat packing business, and feedlot business. I grew up in that kind of atmosphere. And I'm pretty much in the same kind of business myself.

My grandfather was an immigrant from Lithuania, who started out in New York selling shoelaces and headed this way. He was a butcher when he was just a young boy. When he reached the Owens Valley (peddling meat along the way), he would buy a steer and butcher it and sell it on the way. He started a route through the Owens Valley and around to the other end at Tehachapi, down to Bakersfield and the San Joaquin Valley. Then he went into business and worked for a man named Mr. Coleman in the early 1900s in Bakersfield and later formed a partnership in the Kern Valley Packing Company. From there he went to Los Angeles, where he had a hardware store and a grocery store for a short time and then came back and bought the Kern Valley Packing Company from Mr. Coleman. It's been in the family all this time. He built it and expanded on it. They slaughtered cattle, sheep, an' hogs. They also had a sausage kitchen and made bacon an' ham. And that's the business I'm in now; I'm the president of the Kern Valley Packing Company. I bought it, along with some partners, about three years ago now. My granddad was the businessman and very rarely got on horseback, because he wasn't inclined that way. But he had large cattle and sheep holdings all through the desert here and all through the West, actually. They tell a story about my granddad as having said, when he was still a young man, "I'm going to have 12 children and be a millionaire before I die." His first wife died when they had 11 children, but he remarried in his late sixties and had his 12th child, a girl. She's my aunt and younger than I am. She just graduated from law school.

I've had a very full childhood and a very full life, being able to travel all through the West with my dad on business trips and cattle buying trips, working in all different phases of the cattle business — not just in one kind or one area. No two people work cattle alike. The cowboys from one area will work cattle one way, and the cowboys from another area will work cattle another way. And I was exposed to all different facets of the cattle business that way.

I was a farm management major in college at Cal Poly. I graduated from there in 1967. During the time I was in college I rodeo'd and was on the Cal Poly rodeo team, riding saddle broncs and team roping. I liked saddle-bronc riding best. I did pretty good at that. Probably the best ride I ever made was at the college national finals where I won a go-around [tournament winner], I won the first go-around on a horse that had been an old buckin' horse but hadn't been buckin' too good. We put a chain on his halter; it kind of slowed him up a little,

and he really bucked! Everything just jelled, and I made the finest ride of my life against some guys who later were world-champion saddle-bronc riders.

The cowboy I remember as being an all-around top hand is one who just shot himself this summer. His name was Les Jenkins. He lived on this ranch and was the cow boss for the Onyx Ranch for quite a few years when I was here as a young kid. This kind of a person sticks in your mind. He was influential in my training when I was young. I looked up to him. I thought he was one of the best cowboys that I've ever known, and I'd say that was still true today. Les Jenkins was quite an individual. He ran away from home when he was quite a small boy, maybe 12 years old. He told me he was originally from Santa Barbara. His parents grew peas, and they just worked him to death. But he just pulled out when he was 12 years old and never came back. His mother died here maybe five years ago, and after all that time he was still so bitter against his mother that he wouldn't go to her funeral. He studied the cow business and had it down to a science. He knew just what a cow would do in every instance and what a steer would do and what a horse would do. He could tell you what to expect at any time. He was always just a jump ahead of everybody else. I first ran into him on the 3B ranch in Arizona. I was just four or five years old then. That was my first meeting with Les. He came to California to work for us over here after we sold the Arizona ranch, and he stayed on the Onyx Ranch quite a few years. He was a roper and used to rodeo when he was a young man. But Les ended his life just like he lived it.

He had gone to South Dakota to live on some of his wife's relatives' land. They were part American Indian and they were on the Indian reservation. He was running his own cattle there. I guess he was 80-some years old. He had a stroke and was partially paralyzed. He figured that, like a horse with a broken leg, he just wouldn't be good anymore, so he went out in the barn and put a gun to his head and pulled the trigger. He wasn't going to be a burden to anybody. That was his style. You could have predicted it. But he was quite a man.

One time Les and I were out after some cattle. We were trying to gather the remnants from the desert, and we knew an area where there were probably a few cattle running. It was right on top of a peak. The cattle could have gone either the right way or the wrong way, just depending on how we jumped them. We came up over a rise and saw the cattle grazing a few hundred yards down the wrong side of the slope. When they first saw us, they kind of jumped. They were alerted. In my position, I had to get down around the bottom side of them to keep them from going the wrong way. I was a pretty small kid. I held the cattle up just right. Just happened to get lucky and stopped them and headed them back the right way. Les pointed out that I did a good job. It really stuck in my mind to this day, because I wasn't used to getting praise.

Today we have trouble getting cowboys. They're not a very dependable group as a whole, mostly drifters, and that's the way they always have been. But it seems like there are fewer of them around now. They don't take things too seriously, and they are always just movin'

through, movin' somewhere. Lookin' for something else. Either that or somebody's chasin' 'em! The sheriff has been down here a number of times through the years lookin' for cowboys who hadn't paid their alimony or child support. Not really thugs or anything like that. Just people that are movin', trying to keep one step ahead of the law. They're just a different breed. Definitely a vanishing breed. And probably there will come a day when you won't have anybody left that can drive a set of cattle down the road and gather them and keep them in good shape and know how to be in the right place at the right time. Not many cowboys any longer do that with any skill. It takes years of experience.

Now there are too many high-paid jobs in the city. Too many jobs a person can do and make more money doing something else. In the cattle business it's pretty much traditional to pay low wages and not be able to afford to pay any higher wages. So you've lost probably the better men to better paying jobs. That's the one single factor. Cowboys learn to do other things for survival. They learn to do other things besides ride a horse or drive cattle and understand cattle. It's probably easier to learn to ride a bulldozer or a piece of heavy equipment than it is to learn to be a cowboy. And you have fewer people who are willing to give dedication to a job where they're not lookin' at a health plan and a retirement plan and a this-and-that plan. There's a lot of benefits to being a cowboy and living in the country and living around animals. It's a healthy environment.

I'd say that the future of the cattle business is in more intensified ranching, smaller operations — where there are more cattle per acre, irrigated operations, and feedlot operations. The cattle business will always have a place, but it's getting more and more away from a large, grandiose ranch operation to a small deal where a guy could either handle it in a confined situation like a feedlot or he handles it where it doesn't take all the skills of a cowboy to move the cattle and do what you have to with cattle. Yet when I really think about it, the ranches that are in operation today have been in operation over quite a few years under the same kind of circumstances. There's always somebody around that will do it, that will do the work.

All my kids like to ride. I've got three and that's it. But I'm not pushing them. I don't really care if they become cowboys. I just want them to have the opportunity to do what they want and be happy at what they're doin'. So I'm not raisin' a family on near the scale that my dad did. It's not going to bother me if they don't go in the cattle business, but I'd be very happy if they did. I wouldn't live my life any other way.

The cattle business hasn't been enjoyable the last four years, however. It's really been hard. No matter what we did, the cattle would lose money. We'd buy another set and they'd lose money. Everything we did just kept costing money. So it was a tough time. We're out of that now, and we hope that we are not going to have another crash like we did before. To be a good cowboy you have to be a good psychologist. You have to be somewhat of a mechanic. You have to think like cattle, like horses. You have to be able to do just a little bit of everything. I'm sure there are other professions and occupations that take a person of well-rounded skills, but I can't think of one that takes the knowledge and the years it takes to become a cowboy.

DESIGNED BY NANCY SOLOMON
COMPOSED IN LINOTYPE GRANJON
WITH YORK DISPLAY TYPE
PRINTED AT THE PRESS IN THE PINES

NORTHLAND PRESS

BOUND BY ROSWELL BOOKBINDING
PHOENIX